Sainsbury's Homebas

VEGETABLE GARDENING

Joy Larkcom

CONTENTS

NOTES
For convenience, ease of growing symbols have been incorporated in the A-Z sections.
They can be interpreted as follows:
*Easy to grow vegetables
**Vegetables which require more than average care
***Temperamental or difficult to grow vegetables
These symbols are appropriate provided the soil is suitable and fertile.

Published exclusively for
J Sainsbury plc
Stamford Street, London SE1 9LL
by Cathay Books
59 Grosvenor Street, London W1

First published 1983

ISBN 0 86178 1937

Printed in Hong Kong

VEGETABLE GARDEN BASICS: Soils, Manures, Shelter & Planning

There is no use beating about the bush: with very few exceptions, good vegetables can only be produced under good conditions. They need to be grown in an open position with plenty of light and sunshine, and will never flourish tucked away in dark corners, under the shadow of buildings or in the shade of trees. Nor will they do well in an exposed or draughty position (the wind funnels created between high buildings and gaps in garden fences are particularly lethal), and in such situations some kind of windbreak or shelter must be erected to protect the plants.

By far the most important factor, however, is the soil. Vegetables *must* have fertile soil, and the key to successful vegetable growing lies in building up soil fertility. There are many ways in which poor soil can be improved.

A fertile soil fulfils a number of requirements. It has a plentiful supply of plant nutrients or foods – the main ones being nitrogen, phosphorus and potash, and minor but important elements such as calcium, sodium and sulphur. It has a good 'crumb' structure, so that it is pleasant to work, neither solid nor too sandy. It is well drained yet still holds a reservoir of water, and it is well aerated. The oxygen in the soil is essential not just for the plant roots, but also for the millions of micro-organisms that live in the soil and which play a vital role in maintaining fertility.

Soil is made up of mineral particles and humus. The mineral particles (sand, silt and clay) are formed by the weathering of rock, and humus is formed by the breakdown of organic matter – largely decomposing vegetation and animal remains. This decomposition is carried out by the micro-organisms.

It is largely the interaction between the mineral particles and the humus that determines the fertility of the soil. Humus is the agent that enables the mineral particles to form stable crumbs of varying sizes, and it is the spaces between the larger crumbs that form the drainage and aeration system of the soil, draining off surplus water which is then replaced by air. In the smaller spaces between the smaller crumbs, a reservoir of water remains.

Humus is also a rich source of nutrients, and through its interaction with the mineral particles especially the clays, enables them to release nutrients. Humus is really the cornerstone of fertility.

The term 'bulky organic manure' covers a range of products, for example: any animal manure, always as well-rotted as possible, and with as much straw and litter as possible; poultry manure, which is more concentrated so needs to be used sparingly; spent mushroom compost; seaweed, either fresh, dried or composted; treated sewage sludge or municipal waste – in short any kind of vegetable or animal waste. Straw itself can be used, but it should first be rotted down. To do this, make a heap of straw in layers about 15 cm (6 inches) deep, watering each layer, and sprinkling alternate layers with lime and a nitrogenous fertilizer or compost activator. To supplement these manure supplies you should make your own compost.

MAKING COMPOST

Compost must be made in as large a container or bin as possible, so that enough heat can be generated to decompose the material fairly rapidly, and to kill off weed seeds and disease organisms. Compost bins should be constructed on a soil base, ideally providing two boxes side by side, so that one can be built up while the other is in use.

Make them at least 1 metre (3 ft) square, larger if possible. Three sides should be of an insulating material such as brick, timber, or breeze blocks, or if available straw bales. The fourth, front, side can be made of wire panels or removable planks, so that it can be raised and lowered in stages as the heap progresses. In wet areas the compost heap should have some overhead protection.

The starting point is to fork over the soil, then to make an aeration and drainage layer about 8 cm (3 inches) thick, of brushwood, broken bricks, or land drain pipes. It is convenient if strong wire screening (old bed springs serve the purpose well) can be laid over this to support the compost.

ABOVE: Home-made compost bin with timber sides, and stones at ground level for drainage. The heap is built up in layers and covered with perforated plastic and insulating material.
RIGHT: Proprietary plastic compost container. Raw material is put in at the top and compost is removed from the bottom by sliding up the side panels.

Any garden or household refuse which will rot can be put into the compost heap, though it is a sensible precaution to exclude diseased material and weeds that have gone to seed. The compost is best built up in layers 15-23 cm (6-9 inches) deep, preferably building a layer at a time rather than continuously adding small amounts. In small households this is difficult unless refuse can be kept in closed plastic bags until there is enough for a layer.

Large pieces of material such as cabbage stalks should be cut or shredded into small pieces, and different types of material should be mixed together, rather than making a layer of one material only. Grass clippings turn into a soggy mess if put on the heap in one go. Very dry material should be watered.

In the colder months of the year, when there is less nitrogenous green material in the heap, an activator can be added to each layer to stimulate decomposition. This can either be spread on the surface or, preferably, mixed in with the waste. Suitable substances are proprietary activators or concentrated seaweed extracts (in both cases follow the manufacturer's instructions); a sulphate of ammonia or other nitrogenous fertilizers at the rate of 140 g/sq metre (4 oz/sq yd); and poultry or other animal manures at the rate of about a bucketful for each sq metre (sq yard).

Build up the heap until it is about 1.5 metres (5 ft) high, or reaches the top of the bin, then cover it with plastic sheeting which has ventilation holes punched in it and top with an insulating layer of straw, old matting, or a couple of inches of soil.

The temperature in the heap will start to rise, and will then fall. At this point, usually two or three weeks later, decomposition is hastened, and the quality of the compost improved if the heap can be turned (dismantled and built up again), turning the less rotted sides to the middle. The compost should be ready within a few months depending on the season. Good, well-made compost should have the appearance and texture of soil.

WORKING IN ORGANIC MATTER

The humus supply in the soil is used up rapidly, so organic matter has to be added regularly. It is almost impossible to add too much: think in terms of two to three buckets to each square metre, or a layer at least 8 cm (3 inches) thick each year.

Virtually all types of soil are improved by the addition of organic matter. At one extreme are light, well-drained sandy soils which, because they are well drained, lose nutrients rapidly. Humus makes them richer and more moisture-retentive. At the other extreme are heavy clays, cold soils that are difficult to work initially, but intrinsically rich in nutrients. With the addition of humus they become warmer, more easily worked, better drained and more fertile.

Organic matter can be added in a number of ways. On medium to heavy soils it can be done when the soil is dug over in autumn, or when digging between crops. It is considered best to fork the manure thoroughly throughout the top layer of soil, rather than lay it at the bottom of a trench, as used to be advocated.

On very heavy soil another recommended practice is to make the soil into ridges at least 30 cm (1 ft) high in winter, and cover them with a thick layer of manure. The manure protects the soil surface from winter rains, while the frost penetrates the ridges and helps to break down clods. The ridges can be levelled and the manure forked in easily in spring.

Very light soils are best dug in spring to minimize the loss of nutrients in winter rain. So cover the surface with a layer of manure in the autumn, digging it in during the spring.

Well-rotted manure or compost can also be spread on the ground as a mulch, between growing crops, at any time of year. Worms will gradually work it in.

Weed seeds may be introduced into the garden in manure or compost, particularly if the latter is not well made. Although this is a nuisance, the value of the organic matter far outweighs the nuisance of some extra weeding!

FERTILIZERS

In very fertile soils there is no need to use artificial fertilizers, but in the real world, particularly in new gardens, many soils are below par and artificial fertilizers can be used to boost growth. These are either inorganic chemical salts, such as ammonium nitrate, or organic compounds, of which the seaweed based fertilizers are the best value and these often have unexplained but quite marked effects. It must be appreciated that artificial fertilizers have no significant long-term effect on soil fertility, and can therefore only be used to supplement, never replace, organic manures.

Nitrogen, phosphorus, and potash (abbreviated to N, P, and K), are the most important elements applied in fertilizers. Most soils have reasonable reserves of phosphorus and potash, but nitrogen is washed out of the soil during the winter so is most likely to be in short supply. Plants vary in their needs, but leafy crops such as the brassicas and lettuces have high nitrogen requirements; tomatoes need a lot of potash when ripening.

The main nutrients must always be given in balanced form – for example, a nitrogenous fertilizer ought to be balanced with smaller amounts of phosphorus and potash, otherwise the plant's growth will be adversely affected. The simplest way of doing this is to use a proprietary compound fertilizer, which contains N, P, and K in varying proportions.

Fertilizers can be applied in solid form, as dusts or granules which are spread on the ground and watered in, or as liquids that are diluted and watered on the ground. Occasionally they are sprayed on the foliage as a foliar feed (eg some seaweed-based fertilizers), but it unwise to rely entirely on foliar feeding.

Fertilizers are generally used as a 'base dressing', which is raked into the soil just before sowing, or preferably before planting, or as a 'top-dressing' applied during growth. They must be watered in if the ground is dry.

It is impossible to lay down precise rules for feeding, as plant requirements and soil conditions vary tremendously. In an average garden, where reasonable dressings of manure are being applied annually, an annual base dressing of a compound fertilizer, say 10 parts N, 10 parts P, and 10 parts K, at the rate of 60-90 g/sq metre (2-3 oz/sq yd) should be adequate.

MINOR AND TRACE ELEMENTS

Occasionally vegetables fail to grow because of a lack of one of the minor elements or a trace element, the latter being required only in minor quantities. If you are prepared to pay for a professional chemical analysis of a sample of the soil, you will have the deficiency confirmed, and it can usually be remedied by the use of a foliar feed containing the missing element. More often than not trace element deficiencies are caused by over-liming; they are unlikely to occur on well-manured soils.

Two fundamental aspects of soil may affect the fertility unless corrected: soil acidity and poor drainage.

SOIL ACIDITY

Soils have a level of acidity or alkalinity, which broadly speaking reflects the amount of calcium or lime in the soil. Acidity is measured on the pH scale, on which the neutral point is 7. Above pH 7 the soil becomes more alkaline, below 7 it is progressively more acid. The pH can be tested fairly accurately with the soil testing kits that you can buy in garden shops.

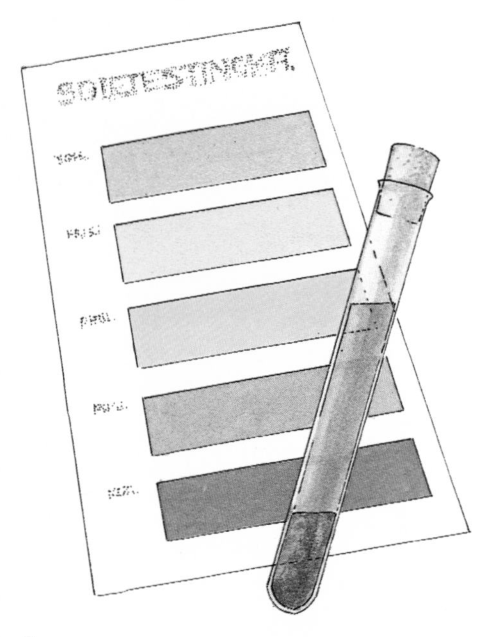

Soil testing kits can be used to test the acidity of your garden soil to see if liming is necessary. They are quite easy to use.

Most vegetables do best on slightly acid soils, at a pH of around 6.5. In the British Isles there is a tendency for soil to become gradually more acid as calcium is washed out during the winter months. This is most marked in industrial areas, in areas of high rainfall, and on light, sandy soils. Clay soils usually have substantial reserves of calcium.

Where vegetables are growing poorly, acidity is frequently the cause; this can be checked with a soil test. Acid soils tend to look sour and mossy, with vegetation lying on the surface rather than rotting. Acidity has to be corrected over the course of several years by liming in the autumn.

To do this, spread ground limestone on the soil before digging – but do not apply manure, or fertilizers containing ammonia, at the same time, as they will interact. An average rate of application would be 550 g/sq metre (1 lb/sq yd), with heavier dressings on clays or extremely acid soils, and lighter dressings on sandy and not seriously acid soils.

DRAINAGE

It is usually obvious when soil is badly drained; water lies on the surface for several days after heavy rain, and is encountered very near the surface when digging. It can be caused by poor soil structure, or by an impenetrable 'hard pan' in the soil, or by the low-lying situation of the land.

Faulty soil structure will gradually be remedied by working in plenty of organic matter. If a hard pan is the cause (this can be created by a mineral layer deposited in the soil, or compaction from heavy machinery), the answer is to dig down to the offending layer and break it physically with a pickaxe.

Where land remains waterlogged, trench drains, which act like a soakaway, can be made across the lower end of the slope. Make the trench about 30 cm (1 ft) wide and two or three times as deep, and fill the bottom half with rubble, stones and so on, before replacing the soil. In most cases this absorbs surplus water sufficiently for the soil to be cultivated successfully. In the few cases where it does not work, a network of underground drainage pipes leading to an outlet will have to be laid by a professional.

Most cases of poor drainage can be remedied by digging simple trench drains across the lower end of the vegetable garden. They should be about 60-90 cm (2-3 ft) deep and half-filled with stones and rubble, which will absorb excess water.

THE RUBBLE PROBLEM

Occasionally one is faced with the apparently hopeless task of building a garden out of builder's rubble. Clear away the largest boulders, buy the largest quantity of manure you can afford and spread it on the ground in a thick layer in the autumn. By the following spring a surprising amount will have worked in, and gardening can begin.

In such a garden start by creating little 'pockets' of fertility, by making miniature trenches about 15 cm (6 inches) deep into which you can work well-rotten compost or commercial potting compost. Sow or plant quick-growing crops such as lettuces, radishes, dwarf beans, and spring onions in these pockets. The mere process of cultivation starts to improve the soil, and you can develop gradually from these beginnings.

SHELTER

As mentioned earlier, vegetables cannot grow well in exposed situations where they are subject to high winds. What is less well known is that even gentle winds can be detrimental: shelter from light winds can increase vegetable yields as much as extra watering or increased fertilizers! So wherever feasible, make the vegetable garden more sheltered.

Trees and hedges may be suitable windbreaks around the perimeter of a large garden, but they are inappropriate in the immediate vicinity of the vegetable garden as they compete for light, water and nutrients.

The ideal garden windbreak is about 50 per cent permeable, so that it filters wind rather than stopping it in its tracks. Lath and wattle fences are good, as are netted windbreaks made from special nylon windbreak materials. These have to be battened to posts, making sure the posts are well anchored as they take a tremendous strain in high winds. A windbreak is effective for a distance roughly two to six times its height – the further from the windbreak the less the effect.

Permanent or temporary low windbreak strips, 30-60 cm (1-2 ft) high, made from netting or hessian sacking, can be put up between crops. Such protection is especially valuable in spring, when strong cold winds prevent young crops from 'getting away'; and in winter, when the combination of low temperatures and cold wind is so damaging.

Where a windbreak is erected across a gap – say in a hedge or between buildings – make it extend several feet beyond the gap on each side. Winds nip around corners very craftily!

GARDEN PLANNING

A vegetable garden can be almost any shape. Traditionally vegetables were grown in large plots in rigid rows, with plenty of space between the rows. Much of the ground was wasted and inevitably trampled over while cultivating and picking the vegetables. Today it is realized that vegetables can be grown much closer together, and very often, instead of being in rows, they are planted in 'blocks' or patches with equidistant spacing between them. This has the additional advantage that the plants form a 'canopy' over the ground, which helps to suppress the weeds.

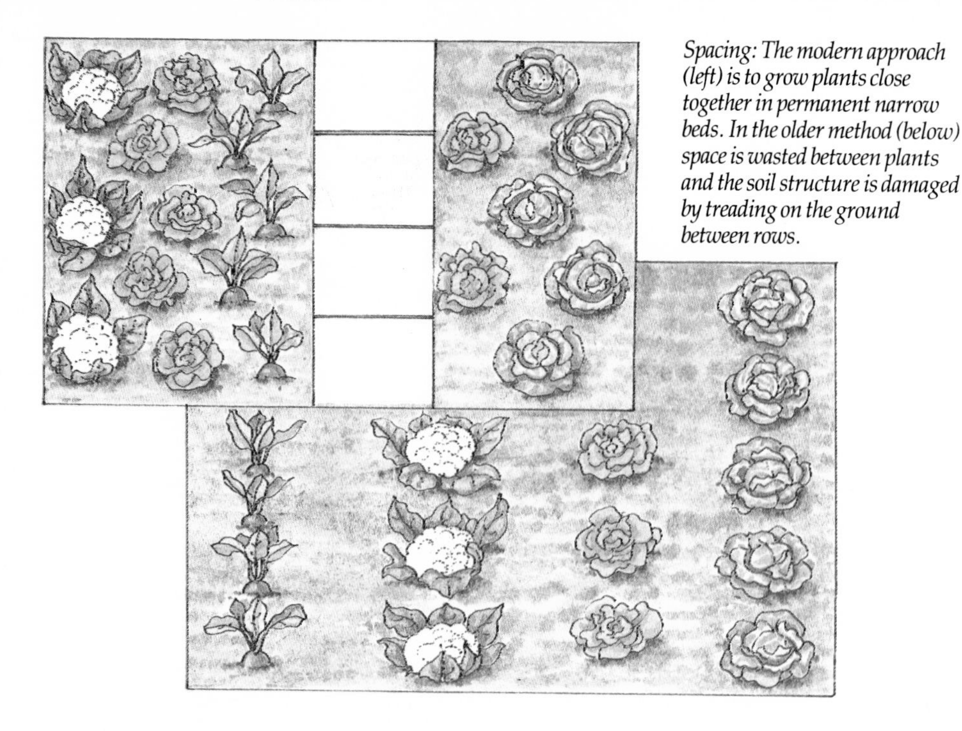

Spacing: The modern approach (left) is to grow plants close together in permanent narrow beds. In the older method (below) space is wasted between plants and the soil structure is damaged by treading on the ground between rows.

Growing vegetables at equidistant spacing lends itself to much smaller beds, which can be accommodated more easily in small modern gardens. Beds 1-1.2 metres (3-4 ft) wide are very convenient, not least because they can be worked from the edge without treading on the soil – and the less the soil is compacted, the better its structure will be.

In small gardens where it is hard to find space for vegetables, a few can be grown in flower beds. Runner beans look very decorative growing up a trellis or wigwam at the back of a border, while beetroot, chards, carrots and the 'Salad Bowl' types of lettuce look pretty growing amongst flowers. The soil, must, however, be rich enough to support them.

The choice of vegetable crops has to be determined largely by family requirements and available space. Few people aim to be self-sufficient, so where space is limited, it is probably not worth growing maincrop potatoes, or vegetables like cauliflowers, which require a large amount of space for long periods. Concentrate instead on salad crops, which are so much better picked fresh from the garden, and unusual but beautifully flavoured vegetables such as calabrese and mange-tout, also called sugar peas, which are rarely on sale and are expensive when they are available.

A big headache is arranging for a continuous supply without gluts and shortages. With the wide range of varieties available today, continuity is much easier to achieve. Wherever possible in the text, suggestions are made for successive sowings of suitable varieties with this in mind. With some vegetables, root crops such as parsnips for example, the whole year's supply can be obtained from one sowing. With others, such as lettuces, carrots, beetroot and cabbages, it is necessary to make several small sowings for a constant supply.

Any keen vegetable grower would be well advised to invest in a cold greenhouse or an inexpensive 'walk in' polythene tunnel. This increases the scope enormously, by making earlier sowings and later harvesting possible. On a smaller scale, cloches and frames can be put to excellent use to extend the season.

A well-planned vegetable garden will provide produce throughout the year.

	Year 1	Year 2	Year 3
Plot 1	A	B	C
Plot 2	B	C	A
Plot 3	C	A	B

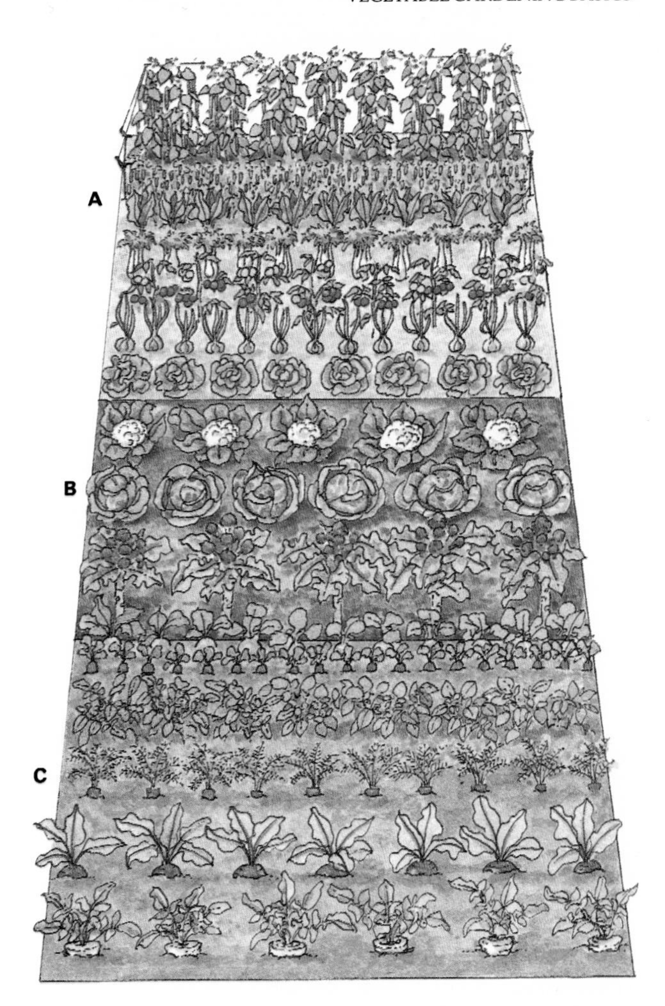

A simple rotation system. The garden is divided into three plots or areas, and the main vegetables grown are divided into three groups. Each group is grown in turn on each plot.
Group A: Legumes, onions, salad crops
Group B: Brassicas (plus radishes, swedes and turnips)
Group C: Root crops eg potatoes, carrots, beetroot, parsnips

ROTATION

It is sound gardening practice to avoid growing the same type of vegetable in the same piece of ground several years running. This is because certain soil pests and diseases, which attack members of the same botanical family, will build up if they have constant access to their host plants.

In practice rotation is a problem in small gardens, but is easier when vegetables are grown in several small or narrow beds rather than a few large ones: there are more permutations.

Wherever possible, try to rotate over at least a three-year cycle. The main family groups which should be grown together in one area then moved on another year are legumes (all the peas and beans), brassicas (all the cabbage family, including swedes, radishes, and turnips); onions and leeks. Important crops like lettuces, potatoes, and carrots should also be rotated.

RECORDS

Keeping gardening records is an essential part of garden planning. Personal records provide invaluable information for future years on the best sowing dates for the area, successful varieties, the quantities required by the household and how to avoid gluts and fill the gaps.

GARDEN ROUTINES: Sowing, Planting, Watering & Protection

SEED SELECTION

Most vegetables are raised from seed, either bought over the counter or from mail order seed houses, whose catalogues are a mine of information. Several developments in seed technology have been of particular help to gardeners, and these include:

F_1 hybrids: These are specially bred varieties that produce exceptionally vigorous and uniform crops. The seeds are more expensive than ordinary 'open pollinated' varieties, but are usually worth the extra cost.

Disease resistance: Several varieties (of tomatoes and cucumbers for example), have been bred with resistance, or at least tolerance, to serious diseases. These can be very useful.

Treated and dressed seed: Seed can be treated by the seedsman to kill diseases that are normally carried on the seed (celery, for instance, can be treated against celery leaf spot). Seed can also be dressed with chemicals to combat soil diseases likely to attack after sowing. Sweet corn and pea seeds are often dressed to increase the chances of success with early out-door sowings.

Pelleted seed: The seed is made into tiny balls with a protective coating, which breaks down in the soil. The individual seeds can be handled very easily and spaced out accurately so that thinning is not required. The ground *must* be kept moist until the seeds germinate.

Foil packaging: Seeds packed in air-sealed foil packs keep fresh much longer than seeds in ordinary packets. Once the packets are opened, however, the seeds deteriorate normally.

CHOOSING A VARIETY

With so many varieties to choose from today, there's bound to be some trial and error before deciding which varieties are best for your conditions and requirements. A few outstanding varieties are mentioned in this book, but there are many others worth growing. Varieties with the Royal Horticultural Society awards can always be relied upon to be of good quality. In order of merit these are FCC (First Class Certificate), AM (Award of Merit) and HC (Highly Commended).

KEEPING SEEDS

Seeds gradually lose their viability, or ability to germinate. In some cases (parsnips, for instance), this happens much faster than in others (radishes, for example). Seeds will remain viable much longer if kept in cool, dry conditions, preferably in air-tight tins or jars. *Never* keep seeds in a damp shed or hot kitchen.

SOWING OUTDOORS

Outdoor sowings are either made directly into the ground where the plant is to grow (generally described as *in situ*) or into a 'seed-bed', which is an area set aside for raising plants; from there they are later transplanted into permanent positions. The main reason for sowing in a seed-bed is to save space. While the seedling is maturing in the seed-bed the ground it will eventually occupy can be used for another crop.

PREPARING THE GROUND

Whether sowing in a seed-bed or *in situ*, the ground has to be prepared for sowing, a process known in both cases, as 'making a seed-bed'.

A seed-bed can only be made satisfactorily when the soil is in the right condition, neither so wet that the soil sticks to your feet, nor so dry that it is unworkable. In spring, especially on heavy soil, it is often a question of waiting until it dries out sufficiently. Putting cloches on the soil can help to dry it out. In very dry conditions the soil may need to be watered before a seed-bed can be made.

The purpose of a seed-bed is to create a surface tilth where the soil is fine enough for seeds to germinate. The underlying soil needs to be firm, but not so consolidated that roots cannot penetrate.

Some soils can simply be raked down in spring and a fine tilth is created with no difficulty. More compacted soils may need to be forked over first, then raked, breaking down large clods with the back of the rake and raking off large stones and persistent earth lumps. Then tread the soil lightly so that it is reasonably firm, and continue raking backwards and forwards until a good tilth is formed.

A well-maintained vegetable patch can be an attractive feature in any garden

Whether sowing *in situ* or in a seed-bed, seeds are normally sown in drills. In a seed-bed the drills are close together, about 10-13 cm (4-5 inches) apart.

Having prepared the seed-bed, mark the position of the row with a garden line and make the drill, which is really just a slit in the soil, with the point of a trowel or corner of a hoe. The depth of the drill varies with the seed: most seeds are sown at a depth roughly two or three times their width. Place the seeds in the bottom of the drill, press them in lightly and use a rake or trowel to cover them with soil.

The golden rule of gardening is to sow seed as thinly as possible. There is always a temptation to sow thickly in case germination is poor. In practice either soil conditions and seed are right and there will be very high germination (and the resulting seedlings may be of poor quality because they are so crowded) or virtually none will germinate and one will have to sow again anyway. So nothing is lost, and everything gained, by thin sowing.

Either space the seed evenly along the drill, or, to save on thinning, sow two or three seeds together at 'stations' several inches apart. Thin to one seedling at each station after germination. If your plants will eventually be grown, say, 15 cm (6 inches) apart, station sow about 8 cm (3 inches) apart. Quick growing seedlings like radishes can be intersown between the stations.

Special steps need to be taken when sowing in extreme conditions. When the soil is very dry, as may happen in mid summer, water the drill only fairly heavily before sowing. Then sow the seeds in the drill and cover them with dry soil. This technique helps to prevent the moisture evaporating, so making sure that the seeds germinate.

Where it is necessary to sow under very wet conditions line the drill with seed or potting compost before sowing.

Thin by nipping off unwanted seedlings just above soil level. This avoids disturbing the remainder.

THINNING

Seedlings grow very rapidly and must never be allowed to become overcrowded. Thin them in stages, so that each just stands clear of its neighbour, until they are the required final distance apart. To avoid disturbing the remaining plants in the row, seedlings can be nipped off at ground level, though in some cases, with lettuce for example, they can be eased out carefully and replanted elsewhere.

SOWING SINGLE SEEDS

Large seeds such as beans, peas, sweet corn, cucumbers, and marrows, can be sown by making individual holes with the point of a dibber. Make sure that the seed lies in the bottom of the hole and is not suspended in air half way down!

BROADCASTING

This is a rapid method of sowing used principally for seeding crops such as cress. Make the seed-bed, then scatter the seeds thinly over the surface. Rake it over first in one direction, then at right angles. Cover the seed-bed with a sheet of polythene or newspaper until the seeds have germinated.

Never sow broadcast on soil known to be full of weed seed: it will be an impossible task separating the weed and vegetable seedlings. In such cases prepare the seed-bed, then leave it for a couple of weeks so that the main flush of weed seeds can germinate, hoe them off and then sow broadcast as described.

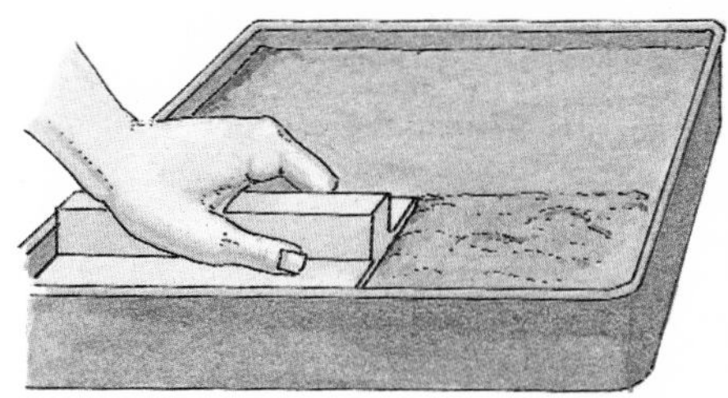

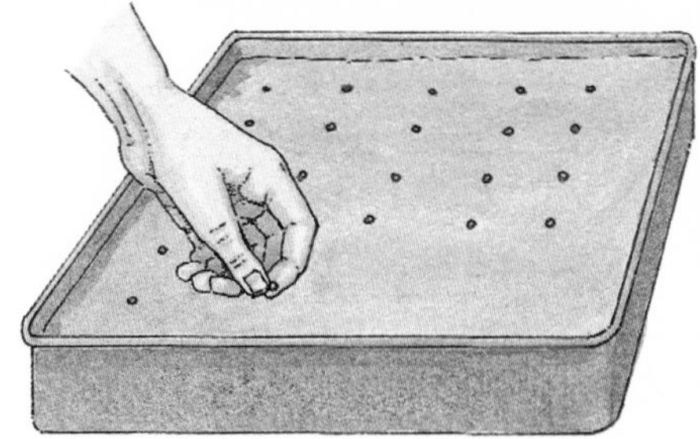

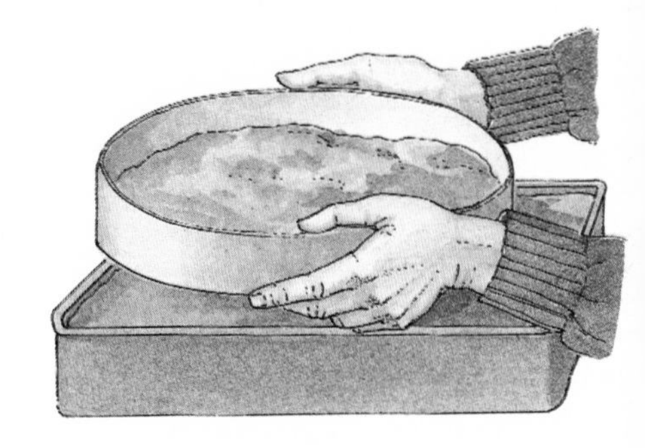

Sowing indoors. The seed tray or pot is filled with moist sowing compost and levelled. The seeds are best sown well spaced out, then covered by sifting more compost over them. The seed tray or pot is then covered with a pane of glass to keep the compost moist until the seeds have germinated.

Crowded seedlings must be pricked out individually into richer compost to give them space to develop further. Hold them by the leaves to avoid damaging the delicate root hairs.

SOWING INDOORS

Half-hardy vegetables like tomatoes and peppers have to be started indoors, otherwise they would never mature in our short summers. With other vegetables, such as celery and lettuces, earlier crops or larger specimens can be obtained by sowing indoors. 'Indoors' implies sowing in a protected environment such as a greenhouse, in frames, under cloches, or even on a windowsill. These early sowings are often made in an electric propagator which provides gentle 'bottom heat', so encouraging germination.

Raising seedlings indoors is simplified by using commercially prepared sowing and potting composts, which are either soil- or peat-based. It is also possible to mix up suitable composts yourself.

Seeds are generally sown in seed trays or pots, but any container with drainage holes made in the bottom can be used. Fill it to within 2 cm (¾ inch) of the top with damp seed compost, firm it with the fingers, and level the surface with a block of wood. Sow the seeds thinly on the surface, spacing them out carefully if only a few plants are required. Cover them by sieving a little more compost over the top, and level the surface once again. If the compost is dry, stand the seed tray in water to absorb moisture. Finally, cover it with a sheet of glass, or pop it into a plastic bag, to keep the surface moist until the seedlings germinate. Remove the glass or plastic for about half an hour a day for ventilation.

Once germinated, the seedlings must be in full light, but not direct sunlight. When they are large enough to handle, generally with about four or five true leaves, they need more room and richer compost. At this stage prick them out into seed trays, or individually into small 6-8 cm (2½-3 inch) pots, filled with potting compost. Water the seedlings beforehand, then uproot them one by one with a small dibber, taking care not to damage the fine roots. Always hold them by their leaves. Make a hole in the compost large enough for the roots, put in the seedling, and firm the soil around it with a dibber. The seed leaves, the first tiny pair of leaves to develop on the stem, should be just above soil level. Space the seedlings 4-5 cm (1½-2 inches) apart, and shield them from bright sunshine until established.

SOWING IN BLOCKS

An excellent but fairly new method of raising plants is to use soil or peat blocks. These are made from potting compost, and are usually about 4 cm (1½ inch) cubes, though they vary in size and shape. Single seeds are sown in the blocks, which can be stood in standard seed trays. The seedlings remain in the blocks until they are ready for planting out, and are planted in their blocks.

The system has many advantages. First, very strong plants are obtained. Their roots spread throughout the block with no competition, and there is very little disturbance when they are planted out. No thinning has to be done, and

Soil or peat blocks are ideal for raising seedlings. A blocking tool is used to make small blocks from special types of potting compost. A seed is sown in each block and develops into a strong plant. When ready, block and seedling are planted out as one with the minimum of root disturbance.

because the blocks are so substantial, they can be planted when the soil would be considered unsuitable, either too wet or too dry, for planting ordinary seedlings. Plants such as Chinese cabbages, which do not transplant well, can be planted successfully if raised in blocks, as the shock is much less than normal.

Blocks are very appropriate for small gardens where relatively few plants are required. Half a dozen each of brassicas, celery, onions, lettuces, bedding plants, and so on, can all be raised in a single seed tray holding about 40 blocks.

The blocks are made with special hand tools, most of which make one block at a time. Use special blocking compost where available (it is more adhesive), otherwise use ordinary potting compost. The compost must be on the wet side to make successful blocks. The tools are designed to make a hole in the top of each block into which the seed is sown. Cover it with compost eased from around the edge of the hole. Large seeds can be handled easily, but small seeds must be tipped singly off a piece of paper. They can also be picked up individually on the moistened tip of a piece of broken glass. When the glass is touched onto the compost, the seed should drop off neatly.

One seed can be sown in each block, or if there is uncertainty about germination, sow two or three seeds in each, nipping off any surplus seedlings at ground level after germination, to leave one in each block.

Keep the blocks moist, especially those made from peat-based compost as the compost is hard to re-wet when dry.

As a makeshift substitute for blocking equipment, ordinary seed trays can be divided into small 4 cm (1½ inch) compartments with strips of cardboard or corrugated plastic. Whatever method is used, the objective is to raise individual plants with no competition and to plant them out with minimum disturbance. This was achieved by the old-fashioned system of raising prize plants in small pots.

Several modern systems offer similar advantages to blocks, for example the pre-formed, polystyrene cellular trays. The cells are filled with potting compost and seeds are sown, or seedlings transplanted into the cells. They develop in the cells until ready for transplanting, when the cell is eased out much like a block.

HARDENING OFF

Before plants are moved into their final position outdoors, whether raised in blocks, in pots or in seed trays, they must be gradually acclimatized to lower temperatures by 'hardening off'. This takes about ten days. Start by increasing the ventilation, then move them outdoors during the day for increasingly longer periods, bringing them in at night, and finally leave them out at night. They are then ready for planting.

PLANTING

Planting is inevitably something of a shock and everything has to be done to minimize the set-back and damage to the plant, especially to the root and delicate root hairs. In most cases the ground is prepared beforehand by forking it over (brassicas, however, can be put straight into un-dug ground). Remove any weeds and rake the surface smooth. The soil should be moist but not saturated; water lightly if it is dry. It is best to plant in the evening, or in overcast conditions.

It is most important that the plants being moved are watered well several hours beforehand, whether they are in a seed-bed, in seed trays or in blocks. Then dig them up carefully with a trowel. Make a hole in the ground large enough to accommodate the roots, and holding the plant in one hand, fill in the soil around the roots, pressing it down with the finger tips. Firm the soil around the stem, then give the leaves a tug. If the plant wobbles, it is not firm enough. If it seems necessary, water the plant afterwards. It is a good idea to mulch (see page 18) at the same time. This both conserves moisture and helps to keep down weeds. If the soil dries out, water lightly every day or so until the plants become established.

In very hot weather young plants, particularly brassicas, are likely to wilt for several days after planting. They can be shaded with home-made conical paper sunhats during this period.

WATERING

Vegetables need moisture throughout their growth, but there are certain times when it is more important than others. Soil must be moist for seeds to germinate, for planting, and when fertilizers are being applied. For different groups of vegetables there are also 'critical periods', when shortage of water is very damaging. Wherever possible, try to ensure that plants are watered at these times.

Leafy vegetables need plenty of water. Mulching helps to conserve water in the soil, by reducing the amount lost through evaporation.

The leafy vegetables – spinach, lettuces, brassicas, celery and so on, are thirsty plants, and benefit from heavy watering throughout their growing season, especially in dry summer months. A weekly rate of 11-16 litres/sq metre (2-3 gallons/sq yd) is sufficient. Their critical period is 10-20 days before maturity. If regular watering is impossible, concentrate on giving one very heavy watering, at twice the rate recommended above, during this period.

The so-called 'fruiting' vegetables include peas, beans, tomatoes, cucumbers, marrows, and sweet corn. These are less demanding in the early stages, but once the flowers appear and the fruits start to form, they need heavy watering. Water them then at a weekly rate of 22 litres/sq metre (4 gallons/sq yd).

Root vegetables have less of a critical period, but if the soil dries out root quality will be poor. When the plants are small, light watering may be needed in dry weather, at the rate of 5 litres/sq metre of row (1 gallon/sq yd). Later in the season, when the roots are swelling, heavier watering at a fortnightly rate of 16-22 litres/sq metre (3-4 gallons/sq yd) is recommended in dry weather.

Water penetrates the soil slowly, layer by layer, and it is much more useful to water occasionally, but heavily, rather than frequently but lightly. Surface watering simply evaporates before it reaches the plant's roots. Always water gently but thoroughly. Large droplets damage the soil surface and young plants, and splash mud up onto the leaves. Use a watering-can, with a fine rose when watering seedlings and young plants. Alternatively semi-automatic systems can be installed, such as the perforated layflat tubing, which is laid along the rows, and garden sprinklers. Water in the evening to minimize evaporation, though in a greenhouse water early enough for the plants to dry before nightfall, so that fungus diseases are not encouraged.

Watering takes time and energy, and in years of drought may be prohibited. Continual watering also washes valuable nutrients out of the soil. So everything should be done to minimize the need for watering by conserving water already in the soil. The best insurance against water shortage is working in plenty of organic matter, which 'holds' the water in the soil. Another valuable practice is mulching, as most of the water in the surface layers of the soil is lost by evaporation not by drainage.

MULCHING

Mulching means covering the soil with a protective layer. This is generally some type of organic material, which will slowly rot into the soil, but over shorter periods plastic film can be used. Mulching both conserves moisture by preventing evaporation and prevents weeds from germinating. It also protects the soil surface from the damaging effect of heavy rain, and from compaction. Furthermore, where organic mulches are used, the worm population is encouraged, and as a result soil structure generally improves.

Many materials can be used for mulching. Their texture is important: they need to be fairly compact but not so compact that moisture and air cannot filter through to the soil. Home-made compost, leaf mould, lawn mowings which have been allowed to dry out first, well-rotted manure, straw and bracken, are all suitable. Provided the plants are not completely swamped, the mulch can be anything up to 10 cm (4 inches) thick.

Ideally you should mulch when the soil is moist and warm. Never mulch when the soil is very dry, very wet, or very cold: it will simply remain that way, providing poor conditions for the plants. The best time to mulch is after planting, or when plants sown *in situ* are several inches high.

A mulch of black polythene helps plants to grow both by conserving the moisture in the soil and by preventing weeds from germinating.

Plastic mulches are useful in the short term, especially for summer crops, such as tomatoes and cucumbers. Either lay the film on the ground and cut cross-like slits through which the plants are planted, or plant first then roll the film gradually over them, making slits and pulling the plants through. Anchor the edges of the film in vertical slits in the soil. Plants can be watered, when necessary, in the gaps around the stem.

Black films are most effective for preventing weed germination, while transparent and white films warm up the soil, the latter reflecting light up onto the plant.

PROTECTED CROPPING

Cloches, frames, greenhouses, and low and 'walk in' polythene tunnels are all devices that can be used to give vegetables extra protection – 'protected cropping', to use the modern terminology. They are invaluable tools for the vegetable grower.

They are effective – partly because they warm up the soil, partly because they protect plants from wind. They will not necessarily protect from frost – only heated greenhouses or frames can guarantee frost protection – but they help to minimize frost damage, which is caused primarily by the lethal combination of low temperatures and strong, cold winds.

Protected cropping is used for earlier sowing and planting. It enables earlier crops of ordinary vegetables such as lettuces and peas, to be grown. It also increases the likelihood of obtaining reasonable crops of half-hardy vegetables such as tomatoes, peppers and aubergines.

The same method is used to extend the season in the autumn, so that later pickings of, say, French beans and radishes can be obtained. It can also be used for ripening tomatoes and onions.

Protected cropping is also used for overwintered seedlings and winter salad vegetables such as endives, corn salad and lamb's lettuce. This improves their quality enormously.

Protected cropping incidentally gives protection against birds and cats!

To get the maximum benefit from protected cropping, the soil must be as fertile as possible, with plenty of well-rotted organic material worked in.

CLOCHES

Cloches are small units made in a variety of materials ranging from glass to plastic. Glass cloches are the most expensive, but breakages apart, are the most durable, give the best light transmission, and absorb and retain heat best. They are, however, heavy to handle and a little awkward to erect. Of the many plastic materials, the double layered corrugated propylene, sold as Correx, provides excellent growing conditions, plants doing well in the somewhat diffuse light they create.

Cloches are easily moved from one crop to another and are often placed end to end to cover a row. Their disadvantages are the labour involved in lifting them for watering, weeding, harvesting and ventilation, and that tall plants outgrow all but the largest cloches.

Stability is important, especially in exposed positions. Cloches are liable to be blown away unless some method of anchorage is adopted (see illustration). The ends should always be closed with a pane of glass or plastic, otherwise a wind funnel is created.

Ventilation is essential in warm and close weather; if there is no built-in ventilation method, move cloches a few inches apart during the day.

Low polythene tunnels are cheaper than cloches and used in much the same way. They consist of polythene film stretched over a series of low, galvanized wire hoops. The film is held in place with fine wire or string stretched from side to side. The ends are anchored in the soil or tied to a stake (see illustration). The sides can be

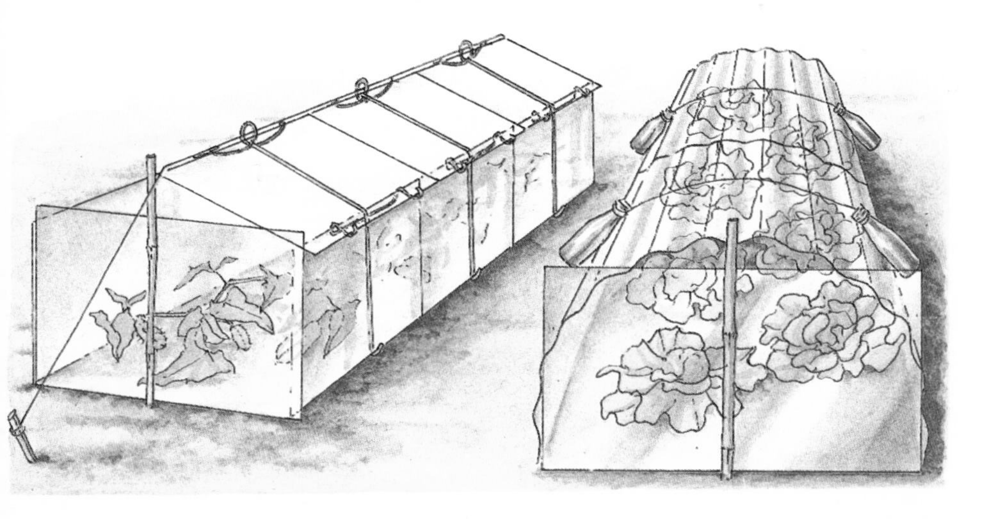

Cloches can be anchored by string run through eyes on the cloche roofs, attached to pegs in the ground (above). Plastic cloches can be held down by plastic bottles filled with water, attached to strings (above). The open ends of cloches must be closed to avoid draughts: use glass or rigid plastic, held with a cane.

Low tunnels made of polythene film stretched over galvanized wire hoops are the cheapest method of protecting plants. The ends of the polythene can be buried in the soil or tied around sticks to secure. The film can be pushed up for ventilation and for weeding, watering, picking etc.

rolled up for watering and ventilation. The film usually needs replacement after two years.

FRAMES

Traditional frames were usually permanent fixtures, with brick sides and glass 'lights' or lids. Modern frames tend to be portable, and constructed of wood, plastic material, or aluminium and glass. They are fairly expensive for the amount of ground covered, and are best used for raising and hardening off plants, for summer crops of half-hardy vegetables such as cucumbers, tomatoes, and peppers, and for winter salad crops.

GREENHOUSES AND 'WALK IN' TUNNELS

Greenhouses are something of a luxury for growing vegetables and are mainly used for tomatoes, cucumbers, and winter lettuces. With heating, earlier crops can be obtained but this has become prohibitively expensive. One drawback is that tomatoes and cucumbers can only be grown for about three consecutive years in greenhouse soil before it becomes disease-ridden. It then has to be completely replaced or sterilized, both laborious and difficult procedures, or future crops have to be grown in uncontaminated soil in pots or growing bags.

For enthusiastic vegetable growers the new 'walk in' polythene tunnels offer several advantages over traditional greenhouses. They are a fraction of the cost, are easily constructed as no foundations are required, and are easily moved to a fresh site in the garden, solving the problem of diseased soil.

A suitable size for a garden is 3 x 6 metres (10 x 20 ft), and about 2 metres (6 ft) high. The framework is made of galvanized tubular hoops, over which polythene film is stretched.

Use strong, 500-600 gauge film, treated with ultra-violet inhibitors so that it lasts at least three years.

Put up the tunnel on a calm, warm day, so that the polythene is limp and can be pulled taut. The hoops are dug into the soil, and a small trench is taken out around the base of the tunnel. The sheeting is pulled over the hoops with the edges lying in the trench; soil is filled in to anchor it.

Doors can be fitted into either or both ends of the tunnel, attaching film to the door frame with battens. Ventilation is most important in polythene tunnels, both in summer and winter, so it is advisable to insert permanent screen panels into the top half of the door. Staging can be constructed inside the tunnel as in any greenhouse. With careful planning, vegetables can be grown in the tunnel all the year round.

'Walk in' polythene tunnels are cheap and ideal for vegetable growing. No foundations are required. The film is held in place by burying the edges in a trench around the base of the tunnel. If the soil becomes diseased the structure is easily moved to a fresh site.

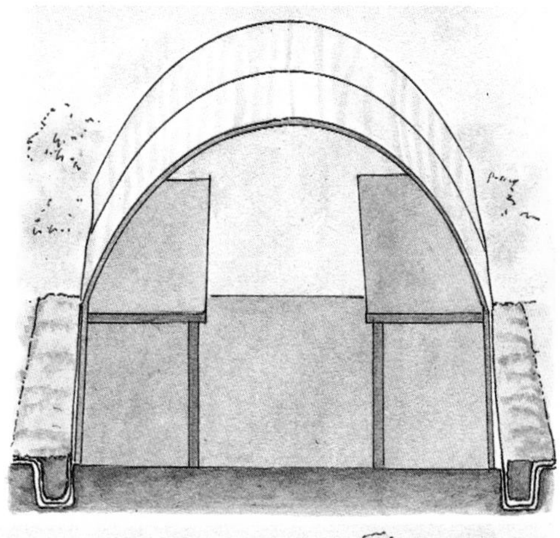

PROBLEMS & REMEDIES: Weed Control, Pests & Diseases

For a successful vegetable crop, it is essential to recognize problems and deal with them as soon as they arise.

WEED CONTROL

Weeds have to be controlled in a vegetable garden because they compete for nutrients in the soil, for moisture, and for light. There are two types: perennials and annuals.

The perennials last from one year to the next by means of very deep roots, or by creeping stems and roots. Common examples are ground elder, bindweed, docks, couch grass and creeping thistle. Once a garden is well established they pose little problem, but in the early stages they have to be dug out manually, making sure that no little pieces of root or stem are left in the soil, as they are very likely to regenerate. Chemical weedkillers may prove useful in clearing a weed-infested site initially. Suitable weedkillers include glyphosate, and dalapon (which is very effective against grasses). They can be applied with a watering-can, using either a rose or a dribble bar. Always follow the manufacturer's instructions implicitly. In some cases it is necessary to leave the ground for several weeks or months before it is safe to sow or plant.

Annuals germinate, flower and die at least once, maybe two or three times in a season, and are far more of a problem. Chickweed, groundsel, shepherd's purse, and annual meadow grass are most common. They seed prolifically, and because weed seeds often remain viable for many years, the proverbial one year's seeding really can mean seven years of weeding. It is essential to prevent them going to seed.

Diluted weedkillers can be applied carefully with a dribble bar attached to a watering can.

They are also best controlled by hand weeding or hoeing. Always hoe as shallowly as possible, to prevent damage to surface roots, and to cut down on the loss of moisture from the soil. In wet weather small weeds may re-root, so should be removed. In dry weather they can be left on the surface to wilt. Weeds that have gone to seed should be burnt.

It is now known that the most competitive weeds are those between, rather than within the rows – so concentrate on removing them first. For a crop sown directly in the ground, competition starts to become really serious two to three weeks after the crop germinates. Start weeding then, if not before! Raising plants indoors gives them a head start over weeds. Also as already mentioned, relatively close, equidistant spacing reduces the light reaching the soil, and is therefore an effective means of keeping down weeds – as is mulching.

Using chemical weedkillers in an established vegetable garden is liable to damage plants, and is not generally recommended.

PESTS AND DISEASES

Although vegetables are bound to suffer from some pests and diseases, in fertile, well-drained, weed-free soil, where careful rotation is practised and watering and feeding are adequate, well-grown plants will outgrow most pest and disease attacks. Pests and diseases flourish in poor conditions, and where plants are of mediocre quality.

From the point of view of raising healthy plants, the early stages are the most important. Always sow in warm conditions so that germination is rapid; sow thinly and thin early so that there is never any overcrowding. Plant out as soon as feasible before the plants become checked in any way, either starved in a seed tray or elongated and drawn in an overcrowded seed-bed. Plant only the sturdiest plants.

Many pests and diseases live through winter in debris and on weeds, so keep the garden clean, burning any rubbish. Handle vegetables for storage very gently, as bruises and even tiny cuts provide a toehold for storage rots. Never force plants unduly particularly under glass. The warmer and 'closer' a greenhouse, the higher the risk of pests and diseases.

Chemical insecticides should be used sparingly in the vegetable garden, as they are likely to kill beneficial predators and pollinating insects as well as pests. Always spray in the evening or in dull weather when pollinating insects are not flying, and under calm conditions, so that spray does not drift unnecessarily. A 1 litre (2 pint) hand sprayer is sufficient for most purposes.

Of the pests and diseases that might attack your crops, the following are the most likely problems to be encountered.

BIRDS AND OTHER ANIMALS

Large birds, such as pigeons and jays, damage brassicas and peas, especially in winter and spring. Bird scarers have some effect provided they are moved frequently. In the last resort the whole garden may have to be netted in.

Small birds, such as sparrows, mainly attack the seedlings of beetroot, lettuces, and peas. Run a single strand of strong black cotton (such as button thread) 6 cm (2½ inches) above the row after sowing. Movable protective netting can be erected over low hoops made of galvanized wire or corrugated plastic strips.

Prowling cats can also damage crops. To avoid this, lay wire-netting or brushwood over seed-beds.

Mice and voles will nibble seedlings and unearth pea seeds. If they really become a problem, set traps, which outdoors *must* be placed in pipes or under tiles.

In rural areas, rabbits can be a nuisance. The only effective protective measure is 60 cm (2 ft) high, 4-5 cm (1½-2 inch) mesh wire fencing around the garden. Bury it, the bottom turned outwards, about 10 cm (4 inches) deep.

SOIL PESTS

Various pests live in the soil, making damaging holes in potatoes and other root crops, and nipping off young plants at soil level.

Wireworms and Leatherjackets: These are two of the commonest soil pests. Wireworms are thin, wiry, yellow larva, 2.5 cm (1 inch) long. Leatherjackets are chubby brown grubs, about 4 cm (1½ inches) long. They are both worst for the first two or three years in newly cultivated ground, but gradually disappear with cultivation, which exposes them to birds – and humans! Pick them up and destroy them. Dig up any wilted seedlings: the pests will often be found on the roots.

Cutworms: These are 5 cm (2 inch) long, greenish-grey or brown caterpillars. In some years

Single strands of strong black cotton, held just above ground level, keep birds off young seedlings.

To protect larger plants netting can be laid over wire or plastic hoops.

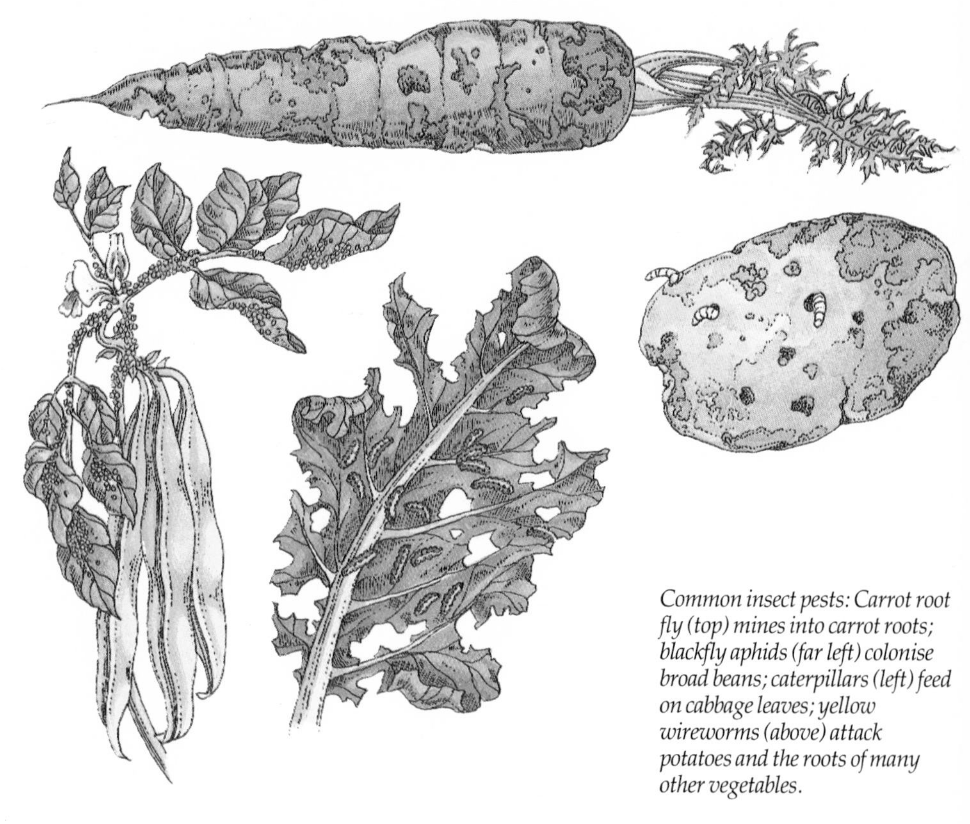

Common insect pests: Carrot root fly (top) mines into carrot roots; blackfly aphids (far left) colonise broad beans; caterpillars (left) feed on cabbage leaves; yellow wireworms (above) attack potatoes and the roots of many other vegetables.

they seriously damage young plants by biting through the stems.

Various chemicals, such as bromophos, can be worked into the top 5 cm (2 inches) of the soil before sowing or planting to control these soil pests. Such chemicals can also kill beneficial soil insects, so they should only be used as an emergency measure.

Slugs and snails: These live in and on the soil, and are worst in wet areas and on heavy soils. They feed at night on a wide range of leafy vegetables. Use slug pellets to control them, or hunt for them at night with a torch, picking them off plants and destroying them.

INSECT PESTS

Although preventive measures are preferable, there are many chemicals for controlling pests. Read the labels carefully to see what is appropriate. Chemicals extracted from plants, such as derris and pyrethrum, are safest to use in the garden. These and other contact sprays such as malathion are sprayed directly onto the insects to kill them. Systemic insecticides such as dimethoate are absorbed into the plant, killing insects that subsequently feed on them.

Aphids: The many types colonize plants suddenly, feeding on the sap. Blackfly attack broad, French and runner beans; greenfly attack lettuces, brassicas, carrots, and other crops; mealy aphids attack brassicas, and so on. They can be controlled with derris, pyrethrum, malathion, or dimethoate.

Caterpillars: These are commonly found on brassicas. Destroy them by hand, or spray with derris or pyrethrum.

Flea beetles: These make round holes in brassica seedlings, especially in dry weather. Spray or dust with derris.

Cabbage root fly: Tiny white grubs cause brassica transplants to wilt and die. Prevent the adult flies from laying eggs by slipping plastic paper cups with the bottom removed over the plants when planting. Or slip discs around the stem, made from flexible material such as carpet underlay about 13 cm (5 inches) in diameter, with a slit from the outside edge to the small central hole.

Carrot fly: Small white grubs attack the roots. Take measures suggested on page 47. Cabbage root fly and carrot fly can also be controlled with the chemicals recommended for soil pests.

In greenhouses, whitefly and red spider mites (seen as a rusty-coloured film on the underside of leaves) can be very persistent pests. Prevent their build up by creating a damp atmosphere coupled with maximum ventilation. They can sometimes, but not always, be controlled by malathion and other recommended chemicals.

DISEASES

Diseases spread rapidly in favourable conditions and are much harder to control, once established, than pest attacks. So any spraying either has to be done in anticipation of attacks, or as soon as the first symptoms are noticed. Even more than with pests, prevention is better than cure. Healthily grown plants, rotation, garden hygiene, and burning all diseased material are of paramount importance.

'Damping off': Fungus infection can prevent seed germinating or cause seedlings to wilt and die when very small. Damping off can be avoided by sowing in warm conditions in clean soil, or by using seed dusted with a fungicide.

Downy mildew: This affects lettuces, brassicas and onions. Grey and white areas appear beneath the leaves. Overcrowding and close, wet conditions are the cause; spray with mancozeb in the early stages of the disease.

Lettuce botrytis or grey mould: Grey mould appears on the leaves, and the plants often rot off at ground level, especially in the winter months. Spray early with benomyl.

Clubroot: This nasty disease affects brassicas, causing swollen galls on the roots. It is soil-borne and hard to eliminate, and is most likely to occur on poorly drained acid soil. Improve drainage, apply lime, and rotate carefully. Dip young plants into calomel or thiophanate-methyl before planting.

Potato and tomato blight: Brown patches appear on the leaves and on tomato fruits, generally in wet seasons in late summer. Spray maincrop potatoes with a copper-based fungicide in early July, and outdoor tomatoes after they have been 'stopped'.

Viruses: This group of diseases, often spread by aphids, has no remedy. They cause stunted growth and discoloured, twisted and mottled foliage. Cucumbers, potatoes, and tomatoes are particularly prone to viruses. Infected plants must be removed and burnt.

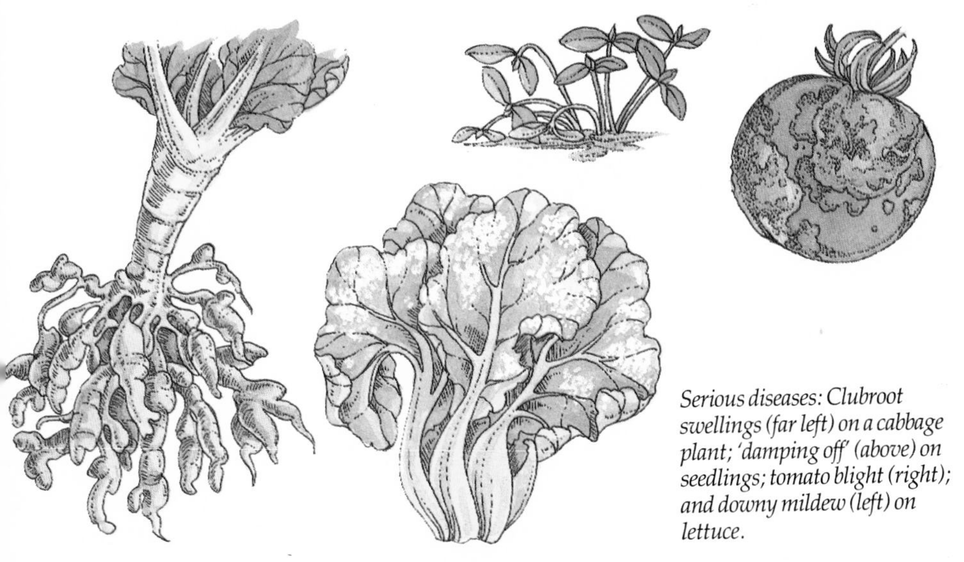

Serious diseases: Clubroot swellings (far left) on a cabbage plant; 'damping off' (above) on seedlings; tomato blight (right); and downy mildew (left) on lettuce.

BRASSICAS

'Brassica' is a general term for vegetables in the cabbage family – cabbages, Brussels sprouts, cauliflowers, kales, for example. Most of them take up quite a lot of garden space and are in the ground over a relatively long period. For this reason, and because they are cheap to buy, it is probably only worth growing them if you have a medium to large garden.

All the brassicas are hungry plants, requiring fertile, well-drained, slightly acid soil and plenty of moisture throughout their growing period. They need an open, unshaded site, but rotate them between different plots of ground on a three- to-four year cycle if possible, to avoid the build-up of soil-borne pests and diseases, such as clubroot. They are best planted on ground that has had plenty of well-rotted manure or compost incorporated into the soil for the previous crop, as a very rich soil will encourage soft growth that is more prone to disease. If the soil is not very fertile, brassicas can be given a top-dressing of a nitrogenous fertilizer, or a seaweed-based liquid fertilizer, during the growing season.

Brassicas are generally raised in a seed-bed and transplanted into their permanent positions when they have three or four leaves. It is often convenient to sow them in soil or peat blocks, as usually just a few plants will be enough for most families.

Plant the seedlings into firm soil (there is no need to fork over the ground immediately beforehand), with the lower leaves just above soil level. It is most important for brassicas to be stable at their roots: it is even worth 'earthing up' the base of the stem as they grow, by drawing soil up around the stem. On very light soils plant them in drills about 10 cm (4 inches) deep, gradually filling in the drill until it is at soil level. The larger brassicas, such as Brussels sprouts and purple-sprouting broccoli, may need to be tied to a stake to prevent them 'rocking' in the wind in winter, especially in exposed gardens.

Brassicas like plenty of water and they should be give 11-16 litres/sq m (2-3 gallons/sq yd) once a week in dry weather. If regular watering is impossible, try to give one very heavy watering of 22 litres/sq metre (4 gallons/sq yd) two to three weeks before they are ready to be harvested. This will pay dividends.

Pests and Diseases: Cabbage root fly is one of the worst of the brassica pests, often attacking the young seedlings shortly after planting out. The plants wilt, then die. A simple but effective measure against attack is to slip home-made 15 cm (6 inch) discs of rubber (foam carpet underlay is ideal) around the stem when planting. Other likely pests are flea beetle, caterpillars and mealy aphids. During spring and winter it may be necessary to net the crop against attacks from birds.

The most serious brassica disease is clubroot. It is most likely to occur on very acid and poorly drained soils – liming to remedy acidity and improving drainage should both help.

BROCCOLI, SPROUTING*

Purple-sprouting broccoli is one of the major standbys of the winter. It is very hardy and prolific. Three or four plants are quite sufficient for the average household. The slightly less common white form of sprouting broccoli is somewhat less hardy and less productive. There are early and late forms of both types, but no named varieties.

Cultivation: Seed should be sown in a seed-bed or in soil or peat blocks from mid April to mid May, starting with the early varieties. Plant out firmly from early June until mid July, spacing the plants 60 cm (2 ft) apart each way. In good soil purple-sprouting plants can grow enormous, so it is advisable to earth up the stems and stake the plants.

Pests and Diseases: Sprouting broccoli is less prone to pests and diseases than most brassicas, the worst enemy being pigeons in winter. Clubroot, cabbage root fly and caterpillars can be problems.

Harvesting: Snap off the flowering shoots when they are about 15 cm (6 inches) long, before the flowers open. Keep picking regularly.

Sprouting broccoli is very suitable for freezing.

BRUSSELS SPROUTS*

We associate Brussels sprouts with Christmas, but by sowing a succession of the modern F_1 varieties, the season can now be extended from September to March. Like purple-sprouting broccoli, Brussels sprouts are among our hardiest vegetables, although they do succumb in the most severe winters.

Cultivation: All varieties should be sown between mid March and mid April. They can either be sown under cloches or in a garden frame (this will produce the earliest crops), or in a seed-bed outdoors. Again, to make transplanting easy, they can also be sown in soil or peat blocks, which can be placed in a garden frame, under cloches, or stood outside.

From mid March to mid April sowing under cover, the following F_1 varieties should provide a continuous supply over a six-month period: 'Peer Gynt' (*September to October*); 'Valiant' (*October to November*); 'Perfect Line' or 'Achilles' (*November to December*); 'Rampart' (*December to January*); 'Fortress' (*January to March*).

Of course you may only want to select one or two varieties from this to meet the household's requirements.

Plant between mid May and early June in firm ground that has not been freshly manured. The standard spacing is 60 cm (2 ft) apart in each direction, a distance that encourages small, uniform sprouts to be ready over a relatively short period. However, if you prefer larger sprouts, maturing over a longer period, plant them up to 90 cm (3 ft) apart.

Full stem of Brussels sprouts ready for harvesting

Apart from watering soon after transplanting to help the seedlings to become established, further watering is rarely required, except under drought conditions. This is because the wide spacing between plants means there is less competition.

Sprouts sometimes become loose or 'blown'. This may be caused by loose soil, by planting in freshly manured ground, or by giving too much nitrogen in the early stages of growth. Make sure the stems are earthed up and the plants staked, and if any extra feeding is done, late summer is the most suitable time.

Early varieties of Brussels sprouts, such as 'Peer Gynt', can be 'stopped', which means nipping out the top of the stem. This encourages the sprouts to button up sooner and to be more uniform in size, so giving earlier picking over a shorter season. It is particularly useful if you want all the sprouts to mature together and to be of an even size for freezing. Stop the plants when the lowest sprouts on the stem are about 1 cm (½ inch) in diameter. To be effective it must be done before the first week in October – and it is only successful with early varieties.

Pests and Diseases: Brussels sprouts are vulnerable to all the Brassica problems, such as clubroot and cabbage root fly.

Harvesting: Pick the sprouts from the bottom of the stem upwards, and do not neglect the sprout 'top' – which can develop almost into a miniature cabbage in spring and is a lovely vegetable in itself. During the winter remove any diseased, withered and yellow leaves from the stem, so that the air can circulate freely around it.

CABBAGES*

There are many excellent modern cabbage varieties, which unlike the old-fashioned varieties stand in good condition for several months once they have matured. This makes it feasible to pick fresh cabbages from your garden all year round. Follow the sowing plan below for a continuous all year round supply of cabbages.

Cultivation: All cabbages can either be sown on seedbeds outdoors and transplanted, or sown in soil or peat blocks or in small pots. You can even sow them direct in the ground and thin them out to the correct spacing. For soil conditions, planting, watering, feeding, and pest and disease control, treat them as recommended for typical brassicas (see page 26). For practical purposes, cabbages are divided into spring (including 'spring greens'), summer, and winter types.

Spring cabbages are sown in late summer and planted in autumn. They can be allowed to form small heads in spring or can be harvested as looser, unhearted plants – spring greens. For headed cabbages space the plants 30 cm (12 inches) apart each way. For spring greens arrange them closer, say 15 cm (6 inches) apart each way, or 10 cm (4 inches) apart in rows 30 cm (1 ft) apart. In this latter case you can use the second and third, fifth and sixth cabbages in the row first (and so on), leaving the remaining plants

CABBAGES

When and how to sow	Which varieties	When to harvest
Spring cabbages Sow directly into the ground in late July and early August; or into a seed-bed for planting out in September	*'Harbinger', 'Avon Crest', 'Offenham' selections*	March to May
Early summer cabbages Sow in heat in late February in blocks or pots, planting out in mid April	*'Hispi', 'Marner Allfruh'*	May to June
Mid-summer cabbages Sow in a garden frame in late March, planting out in late May	in order of maturity: *'Hispi', 'Marner Allfruh', 'Stonehead', 'Market Topper', 'Minicole'*	July to September
Late summer cabbages Sow outside early May, planting June	*'Stonehead'*	September to November
Early winter and/or storage Sow outside late April, planting in early June	*'Hidena', 'Jupiter'*	November to December
Hardy winter cabbages Sow outside mid May, planting towards the end of June	*'Avon Coronet', 'Celtic', 'Celsa', 'Aquarius'*	December to February

30 cm (1 ft) apart to heart up. Varieties such as 'Durham Early' and 'Avon Crest' are particularly suitable for use as spring greens.

Spring cabbages should be earthed up during the winter, and given a feed in March or April if they are looking 'peaky'. Don't, however, feed them when they are planted out, otherwise they will be too 'soft' to withstand the winter. They will survive all but the most severe winters.

Summer cabbages are sown in spring. They are larger, and should be spaced 30-35 cm (12-14 inches) apart each way if you want smallish heads, and up to 45 cm (1½ ft) apart for larger heads.

Winter cabbages come in several distinct types. The Dutch winter white types are excellent fresh or in coleslaw, though they are not very hardy. They can, however, be lifted in November and stored in an airy, frost-free shed, or even in a garden frame – in which case place them on wooden slats, and cover them with a thick layer of loose bracken or straw. Inspect them from time to time and gently rub off any outer leaves which show signs of rotting.

The hardier types, which can be left in the ground all winter, include the crinkly-leaved savoys, the flat, reddish 'January King' type, and newer hybrids between savoys and winter whites. Plant winter cabbage about 20 cm (16 inches) apart if you want small heads, 45 cm 1½ ft) apart for medium sized and 50 cm (20 inches) apart for large heads.

Red cabbages are traditionally grown for pickling, but they also make a superb fresh vegetable, especially if cooked gently with chopped apple, onion, wine vinegar, and a little brown sugar.

Sow red cabbages in March and April, planting out 60 cm (2 ft) apart in May and June. Lift and store any remaining heads in November. Good varieties are 'Langendijker Red' and 'Ruby Ball'.

Pests and Diseases: Cabbage root fly, mealy aphids and cabbage white butterfly caterpillars are frequent pests. Clubroot is a disease that will seriously affect cabbage yields on infected land.

Harvesting: With the exception of a few modern varieties, spring and summer cabbages will stand for only a few weeks once mature, before they start to bolt or otherwise deteriorate. They should be eaten in their prime. If the ground is not required for another crop, cut off the heads, leaving a few inches of stalk in the ground. Make a shallow cross, about 5 mm (¼ inch) deep, in the top of the stalk. Provided the ground is fertile and moist, a second crop of cabbages, sometimes as many as five more heads together on the same stalk, may be obtained.

Non-hardy winter cabbages must be cut before frost, or, with appropriate varieties, lifted and stored before frost. Hardy varieties can be left in the ground until required.

Neat patch of summer cabbages with uniform, firm heads

CABBAGES, CHINESE**

Chinese cabbage is becoming a very popular vegetable, and is certainly worth growing if you like something different. It takes up less space, and has a shorter growing season, than our native brassicas. There are barrel-shaped and pointed-headed types, the leaves being characterized by a very large, crunchy midrib, and prominent white veins. The natural season for Chinese cabbage is later summer to autumn, making it an ideal crop to follow early potatoes or peas. Earlier in the year, due to its response to day length, it is likely to bolt rather than form a head, but the excellent F_1 varieties 'Tip Top' and 'Nagaoka' are in this respect a great improvement on other varieties.

Cultivation: The best time to sow Chinese cabbages is between mid June and mid August. Make several small successive sowings to prolong the season, as the plants tend to mature about the same time from one sowing, and normally don't stand long after maturity before they run to seed. Chinese cabbages have a shallow root system and dislike being transplanted, so either sow direct in the ground, thinning the plants to 30 cm (1 ft) apart in each direction, or sow in soil or peat blocks or small pots, planting out when the seedlings have three or four leaves.

The key to success with Chinese cabbage is to grow it rapidly: it can be ready nine to twelve weeks after sowing. It must have fertile, well-drained, slightly acid soil, with plenty of organic matter worked into it beforehand. The other important factor is moisture – its natural habitat is semi-tropical marshland. Keep the plants mulched to conserve moisture, and water heavily in dry weather.

Pests and Diseases: The normal range of brassica pests and diseases attack Chinese cabbages, but the worst pests are slugs. Take precautions against them, especially in wet summers and autumns.

Harvesting: When the heads are ready, cut them off a couple of inches above ground level, leaving the stump in the ground. They often throw out further useful leaves, though they will not form a substantial second head. The plants will not stand heavy frost, but if you give them cloche protection in autumn, they may well last into December in mild winters. The cut heads will keep for several weeks in a refrigerator if wrapped in polythene. Unlike English cabbages, Chinese cabbages should only be cooked very lightly, otherwise their delicate flavour is destroyed. They are also excellent shredded and used raw in salads.

Mature Chinese cabbages – an increasingly popular vegetable

CALABRESE**

Calabrese, also known as green or Italian sprouting broccoli, is something of a gourmet vegetable, attractive looking with a beautiful flavour. Moreover it is an excellent vegetable for freezing. It has several other merits: it grows fast, sometimes being ready less than three months from sowing; it can be planted very closely; and it requires a less fertile soil than most brassicas.

The best heads are obtained if calabrese can be sown directly in the ground, to avoid the check of transplanting. Sow two or three seeds together at the required distance apart, thinning to one in each position when the seedlings have germinated. Otherwise sow in soil or peat blocks, or if there is no alternative, in a seed-bed, transplanting very carefully while the plants are still small.

The calabrese season lasts roughly from July to October, if several sowings are made, but the plants are killed off by frost. Make the earliest sowings in late March or early April with the variety 'Express Corona'. Sowing can continue in May, June and early July, using the varieties 'Express Corona', 'Green Comet', 'Green Duke', or 'Premium Crop'. These varieties all take different lengths of time to mature, so it is quite feasible to sow several of them at the same time to obtain a succession for the kitchen.

Cultivation: Unlike cabbage, calabrese is very insensitive to planting distances, although the heaviest yields of good quality spears are obtained by planting so that you have 12 plants to a sq metre (2 to a sq ft). Convenient spacing is 15 cm (6 inches) apart in rows 30 cm (1 ft) apart. If the crop is grown for freezing it can be planted closer, say 20 cm (8 inches) apart in each direction. This has the effect of suppressing the sideshoots and making smaller terminal heads, all of which are ready at much the same time.

Calabrese does poorly if checked, so make sure there is always plenty of moisture, watering as suggested earlier for brassicas. This is another case where it is beneficial to keep the soil mulched.

A somewhat different type of calabrese is the variety 'Romanesco'. It has large heads with a purplish tinge – and an outstanding flavour. Sow it in April or May, planting out 60 cm (2 ft) apart in June or July. Harvest from July onwards.

Fine heads of calabrese, also known as 'green broccoli'

Pests and Diseases: As far as pests are concerned calabrese is susceptible to the normal run of brassica pests and diseases, but caterpillars are particularly troublesome. They conceal themselves inaccessibly in the crevices of the spears. Soak the head in salted water for an hour or so before cooking to force them out into the open!

Harvesting: Always cut the main, terminal head of calabrese first, while it is still firm and compact. Smaller lateral spears will then develop so that picking can often continue over a fairly long period.

Large robust cauliflower with firm white curds

CAULIFLOWERS**

There are cauliflower varieties for every season of the year, but as the winter and spring types (both previously known as 'winter broccoli') require a lot of space over a long period, people with smallish gardens are probably best to restrict themselves to early and mid summer cauliflowers, and/or mini-cauliflowers.

Cultivation: There is no escaping the fact that good quality cauliflowers can only be produced under good conditions. They must have deeply dug, fertile soil, preferably on the slightly alkaline side. Very acid soil should be limed. The secret of success with cauliflowers is to try to encourage steady growth without checks of any kind. Plenty of water is a most important factor.

To minimize the transplanting check, cauliflowers are best raised in soil or peat blocks, or small pots, or sown directly in the ground and thinned to the appropriate distance apart. If they have to be sown in a seed-bed, plant them out as young as possible.

Cauliflower curds are very delicate and easily damaged by exposure to the elements. Summer cauliflowers can be protected from the sun, when nearing maturity, by bending a leaf over the head. Winter and spring cauliflowers suffer most if they thaw out rapidly, due to exposure to the sun, after frost. This can be avoided by bending the stem over to the north and earthing it up on the south side.

Sowing times, planting distances, and suitable varieties for the different seasons, are given below.

Early summer cauliflowers: These are ready between mid June and mid July. Either sow them in a garden frame in early October, planting them outdoors in March, or sow them in heat in mid January, harden them off, and plant them out in March, 53 cm (21 inches) apart each way. Suitable varieties, in order of maturing, are 'Alpha', 'Mechelse Classic', and Dominant'.

Mid and late summer cauliflowers: The mid-summer ones mature between mid July and mid August. They can be sown under cold glass in March, planting out in mid May. Late summer cauliflowers, ready for use in late August and September, are sown in late April and are planted out in mid June. Varieties 'Nevada' and 'Dok – Elgon' are suitable for both these crops, planted 53 cm (21 inches) apart each way.

Autumn cauliflowers: These mature between September and November, and are sown in mid May, planting out in early July about 60 cm (2 ft) apart each way. Suitable varieties, in order of maturity, are 'Flora Blanca' and 'Barrier Reef'.

Winter cauliflowers: This type can only be grown in very mild, South West coastal areas, for use in winter and early spring. Sow them in early May, planting out in late July, 68 cm (27 inches) apart each way. Suitable varieties are 'St. Agnes' (maturing late December to January), 'St. Buryan' (for February and March) and 'St. Keverne', (for late March and April).

Spring cauliflowers. These overwintering cauliflowers, maturing between March and late May, need hard conditions and are therefore unsuitable for South West coastal areas. Sow them in late May, planting them out in late July. Suitable varieties, in order of maturity, are 'Angers No 2 – Westmarsh Early' the 'Walcheren Winter' varieties 'Armado April', 'Markanta' and 'Birchington', and 'Angers No 5'.

Mini-cauliflowers. Mini-cauliflowers are tiny curds, 4-9 cm (1½-3½ inches) in diameter, which make handy single portions and are useful for freezing whole. They are obtained by growing early summer cauliflower varieties very close together, planted in square formation 15 cm (6 inches) apart in each direction. Sow in succession from the third week in March until early July, for supplies from the end of June until the end of October. These, of course, take up far less ground space, and mature much faster, than normal-sized cauliflowers.

Pests and Diseases: Clubroot is the most serious disease, and cauliflowers are vulnerable to the same pests as other brassicas. Caterpillars are a particular problem because they can hide in the curd.

KALE*

The kales are especially valuable in the colder parts of the country because they are exceptionally hardy – though it must be said that most people find them rather too coarse. (Pigeons may feel the same, for they rarely attack kale.)

There are broad-leaved and curly-leaved kales – the latter also known as Scotch kale and borecole. With the broad-leaved kales it is the young shoots, produced in spring, that are eaten. With the curly types, the leaves are eaten in winter and the shoots in spring. Kales tend to be rather large plants, but the dwarf varieties of curly kale, such as 'Dwarf Green Curled' and 'Frosty', are suitable for small gardens. The multi-coloured 'ornamental' kales are beautiful plants, and add a wonderful touch of colour to the winter garden. Contrary to general belief, they are edible – though not highly productive.

Cultivation: Kales tolerate poorer soils than most brassicas, though give of their best in fertile soils. Sow them in April and May in a seedbed, planting out firmly in June and July, dwarf forms 38 cm (15 inches) apart, taller varieties 60-75 cm (2-2½ ft) apart. These may need staking. Kales can be fed in spring to encourage the production of fresh shoots.

Pests and Diseases: Kales are susceptible to the same problems as other brassicas, although they are less prone to clubroot. Caterpillars are usually the main problem.

Harvesting: Take only a few leaves at a time from any one plant, rather than stripping it. In spring snap off the shoots when they are 10-12 cm (4-5 inches) long; the plants will continue to grow and crop over several weeks.

Curly-leaved kale – one of the hardiest brassicas

LEAFY VEGETABLES

The dark green leafy vegetables such as spinach and leaf beet are among the most nutritious vegetables, being an excellent source of protein, besides supplying vitamins and minerals.

What is confusing about spinach and related plants is their names. Several completely different plants are popularly known as spinach, while the leaf beets enjoy a bewildering range of names – all in common use.

In practice these leafy vegetables fall into two main groups: the true spinaches, and the leaf beets. The true spinaches are fairly small-leaved annuals which run to seed rapidly. Some people believe they have a better flavour than the leaf beets; that's probably arguable, but they are certainly harder to grow!

The leaf beets, which include Swiss chard or seakale beet, and perpetual spinach – also known as spinach beet or silver beet – are really types of beetroot in which the leaves rather than the roots are the parts eaten. The leaves are much larger and more substantial than spinach leaves, and usually have an enlarged broadened midrib and bulky leaf stalks – all of which are edible. When cooking it is best to strip off the green part, which requires only minimal cooking, and to cook the leaf stalk and midrib, which require longer cooking, separately. Two vegetables for the price of one. The leaf beets are biennial, normally not running to seed until their second season, which means they tend to be useful over a longer period than spinach.

A third type of spinach is New Zealand spinach, a sprawling, half-hardy perennial that tolerates poor soil and dry conditions.

With the exception of New Zealand spinach, spinach and leaf beet must be grown on fertile soil with plenty of organic matter worked in beforehand. Very acid soil should be limed. An abundance of organic matter ensures that the soil is well drained, and that it retains moisture in hot weather – two key factors in growing healthy spinach and leaf beet. It cannot be over-emphasized that lush leafy vegetables can only be obtained by growing the plants well under good soil conditions.

Frequent watering throughout growth encourages good yields, and mulching is always beneficial to help preserve moisture in the soil. If the plants are looking unhealthy, an application of a general fertilizer, or a nitrogenous fertilizer such as sulphate of ammonia, or a seaweed-based fertilizer, can be given during the growing season.

Leafy vegetables can be grown in light shade, and are useful for intercropping between rows of taller plants, such as beans or peas.

All leafy vegetables can either be sown in drills in the ground and thinned to the correct distance apart, or sown in seed trays, or preferably soil or peat blocks, planting out when the seedlings have four or five leaves. The main enemy at this stage is birds, notably sparrows. Provide protection if necessary (see page 23).

LEAF BEETS*

Both perpetual spinach and Swiss chard are useful crops, being productive, reasonably hardy, and much less prone to bolt than spinach. Perpetual spinach is more widely grown than Swiss chard, but has less pronounced midribs, smaller stems, and crops less heavily.

There are several coloured varieties of Swiss chard, the best known being rhubarb chard, which has bright red leaves and stems. Besides its culinary value, it is decorative – as are all the chards.

For the main summer crop of leaf beet, sow in March or April in rows 38-45 cm (15-18 inches) apart, thinning to 30 cm (1 ft) apart in the rows. Give cloche protection during the winter. These plants may well crop from early summer until the following spring. A second sowing can be made in July to provide succession.

Pests and Diseases: Leaf beets are rarely troubled by pests or diseases, but aphids are occasionally a problem.

Harvesting: Cut the stems 2.5 cm (1 inch) or so above ground level. The plants will continue to throw out more leaves over a long period.

Perpetual spinach or 'spinach beet' with its succulent leaves

SORREL*

Sorrel deserves to be much more widely grown, not least because it is one of the vegetables most likely to succeed in neglected and poor gardens. A good patch of sorrel can provide pickings almost all the year round, and only a small quantity is required. It takes only a handful of the sharp lemon-flavoured leaves to make sorrel soup, or to turn an ordinary lettuce salad into something special. As for cooking, it is best cooked lightly together with spinach or one of the leaf beets, in the absolute minimum of water. The combination brings out the best in both.

There are several types of sorrel. Common sorrel has long, arrow-shaped leaves, and grows about 60 cm (2 ft) high; the broad-leaved French sorrel has thicker leaves and grows up to 90 cm (3 ft) high, while the heart-shaped Buckler-leaved sorrel is more of a ground-cover plant. They are not fussy about soil, and do well in both full sun and light shade. It is worth having a few plants in each position; those in the sun will tend to be earliest but will be tough by mid summer, whereas those in the shade will come in later but remain tender longer.

Cultivation: Sorrel is a perennial and it is simplest to grow it in a semi-permanent bed, making a new bed on a fresh site every three or four years. Alternatively it can be treated as an annual, sowing each spring and pulling the entire plant for use.

Sow in March or April, either direct in the ground or in seed trays. If making a permanent bed allow 25-30 cm (10-12 inches) between plants. If growing for one season only the plants can be spaced 10 cm (4 inches) apart. They are trouble-free and require little attention, other than cutting off the seed-heads as they appear.

In cold parts of the country it is worth protecting them with cloches in winter. This may make it possible to continue picking all winter. If the plants do die back, however, they are amongst the earliest to shoot out again in spring, often providing welcome greenery in February. If you want to be sure of winter pickings, lift a few roots in late autumn and plant them up in boxes, or in the soil in a cold greenhouse.

When it comes to renewing the bed, either start again from seed, or divide up the roots of mature plants in spring or autumn, replanting them in a fresh site. You can also leave a good, strong plant to run to seed. Provided the ground is moist, self-sown seedlings will appear in the autumn and spring, and these can be planted into a new bed.

Pests and Diseases: Sorrel is unlikely to be troubled by pests or diseases.

Harvesting: Picking can start once the plants have four or five leaves, usually three or four months after sowing. After the seed-heads are cut back in early summer further growth will normally take place, to provide summer, autumn and winter pickings.

SPINACH**

Spinach is very sensitive to day length, which is why it is apt to bolt in the long days of summer. It does best in autumn, winter and early spring, when steadier growth allows several pickings.

Cultivation: For a summer supply between May and October, frequent small sowings are advisable, as in general only one cut can be made before it runs to seed. In warm parts of the country, the first sowing can be made under cloches in February, followed by outdoor sowings in March. Make further sowings at two- to three-week intervals until July. For these summer sowings use varieties such as 'Longstanding Round' and 'Sigmaleaf'. Sow 1-1½ cm (½-¾ inch) deep, in rows 30 cm (1 ft) apart, thinning to 15 cm (6 inches) apart.

Winter spinach, which can be cropped between October and May, is sown in August and September. Suitable varieties are 'Greenmarket',

Spinach – successive sowings provide a constant supply

'Sigmaleaf', and 'Broad Leaved Prickly'. In this case thin to 23 cm (9 inches) apart. The plants will be of a much better quality if they can be protected from the weather by covering them with cloches in October or November.

Pests and Diseases: Although generally trouble-free, downy mildew can sometimes be a problem. Blackfly or greenfly may also attack occasionally.

Harvesting: Leaves can be eaten very small or allowed to grow larger. Pick them individually off the plant as required. The plants will make further growth, unless conditions cause them to bolt instead.

SPINACH, NEW ZEALAND**

This is a useful vegetable for dry soils, and can be cropped regularly over a long period.

Cultivation: New Zealand spinach is a half-hardy vegetable. It must either be sown indoors in April, hardened off and planted out in May after risk of frost, or sown directly outdoors in mid May – or a little earlier under cloches. To assist germination soak the seed in water overnight before sowing. Space plants about 45 cm (1½ ft) apart in each direction, allowing them room to sprawl over the ground. Although useful for dry, sunny corners, New Zealand does equally well under normal conditions. It will continue growing until frost kills it, and will often seed itself, reappearing the following year.

Pests and Diseases: It is unlikely to be troubled by any serious pest or disease.

Harvesting: New Zealand spinach must be picked regularly, otherwise it becomes tough, and knobbly seedheads are formed. Cut young shoots from the base of the plant and strip off the leaves, discarding the stems.

New Zealand spinach, with its thick, fleshy leaves

LEGUMES

Legumes are the podded vegetables, peas and beans, which give us some of the tastiest and most appreciated produce from the garden. Most of them can be used fresh, deep frozen or dried. On the whole they require reasonably fertile soil with plenty of organic matter in it, so that it is well drained but also retains moisture. It is wise to rotate the legumes in the garden over a three-year cycle if possible, as there are various soil-borne root rots that can build up if legumes are grown continuously on one site.

Peas, broad beans and runner beans are unusual in that they have nitrogen-fixing nodules on their roots, visible as tiny 'blobs', which 'fix' atmospheric nitrogen in the soil for the plant's own use. In most cases this means that it is unnecessary to give them much extra nitrogenous fertilizer.

A lot is now known about the water requirements of legumes. Their 'critical period' for water is during flowering and when the pods are forming. If possible, unless the weather is very wet, give them 5-11 litres/sq metre (1-2 gallons/sq yd) weekly during this time. If this is not possible, concentrate on giving them at least one heavy watering at this rate when the first flowers start to open, and another when the pods are swelling. Unless the weather is exceptionally dry it is unnecessary to water earlier: over-watering in the early stages promotes leafy growth at the expense of the pods.

If you want to save some dry peas and beans for winter use, select a few good plants and leave them unpicked during the season. When the pods have dried to a brown state, pull up the plant by its roots and finish the drying process by hanging it up in an airy shed or greenhouse. Once the pods have dried enough to snap open, take out the peas or beans and store them in airtight jars.

BROAD BEANS*

Broad beans are relatively easy to grow and hardy enough to overwinter to provide an early crop in all but the coldest areas.

Cultivation: Broad beans are deep-rooting plants requiring plenty of moisture, so prepare the ground by digging it as deeply as possible and working in plenty of organic matter. The summer crops require an open site, though the autumn-sown, overwintered plants will benefit from a more sheltered position.

The first sowings can be made in the open in February, with further sowings until May. The seeds are large, and should be sown 4-5 cm (1½-2 inches) deep, either in drills, or in single holes with a dibber. Just make sure the seed touches the bottom of the hole and is not suspended in air. Space them about 23 cm (9 inches) apart each way, either in staggered rows, or in blocks four or five plants wide – which makes economical use of the ground.

For the earliest spring sowings use the tall, long-podded varieties, such as 'Imperial Green Longpod' and 'Exhibition Longpod', which are very hardy. For the later sowings use the broader, shorter-podded 'White Windsor' and 'Green Windsor' varieties, which are said to have better flavour.

Except in the coldest parts of the country, broad beans can also be sown in October and November to provide the first spring pickings. Use the variety 'Aquadulce' or the dwarf variety 'The Sutton'. These sowings can be protected with cloches. 'The Sutton', incidentally, can also be sown in spring, and is a very useful variety for small gardens. An excellent old-fashioned variety, which can also be sown in spring or autumn, is 'Red Epicure'. The pods and beans have a purple tinge, and excellent flavour.

The taller varieties of broad beans can become rather top-heavy and may need support. Put canes at the corners and midway along the blocks or rows, and run strings between them. Wire-netting can also be used as support.

Pests and Diseases: The commonest pest is blackfly or black aphid, which colonizes the growing points. The best remedy is to nip off the tips of the plants once they are flowering well. This not only discourages the aphids, but

encourages the development of the beans.

Harvesting: Beans are ready from about May onwards. Pick the pods before the beans have toughened; they are much better when young. The very young pods can be sliced and cooked without shelling. The young tips can be cooked as 'greens'; mature beans can be dried for winter use.

FRENCH BEANS**

French beans are a versatile crop. We normally eat the immature green pods, either whole or sliced. When the pods are larger they can be shelled and the young green beans inside eaten as 'flageolets'. Finally the mature podded beans can be dried for use during winter.

There are many shapes of bean, ranging from the flat-podded ones, which become stringy when old, to the round, pencil-like varieties such as 'Loch Ness' and 'Tendergreen', which are less stringy and excellent for freezing. If it's flavour you are after,

Tall long-podded broad bean plants, which require support if they become top heavy.

Dwarf French beans ready for picking

try the Waxpods, such as 'Kinghorn Wax', or the purple varieties, such as 'Royal Burgundy'. Both dwarf (bush) and climbing varieties are available; the latter require supports during growth, just like runner beans.

Cultivation: French beans love warmth and hate an exposed, windy position or cold, wet soil. They do best on rich, light, well-drained soil.

Most failures stem from sowing them outdoors too early in cold conditions. The seeds will not germinate until the soil temperature reaches about 10°C (50°F), generally about late April or early May in southern England. Early sowings also suffer a high mortality rate from soil-borne pests and diseases. This can be avoided by sowing indoors. Start by standing the seeds overnight on moist blotting paper until they swell. Then sow them in soil or peat blocks, seed trays or small pots. Plant them out, after hardening off, when 5-8 cm (2-3 inches) high. It sounds

FRENCH BEANS		
When and how to sow	**Which varieties**	**When to harvest**
Sow in a cold greenhouse in mid April, harden off and plant out early June	*Dwarf: 'The Prince', 'Tendergreen'*	late June and July
Sow under cloches in mid April, keep plants covered until June	*Dwarf: 'The Prince', 'Tendergreen'*	July and August
Sow outdoors in mid May and mid June	*Climbing: 'Loch Ness'* *Dwarf: 'Tendergreen'*	late July to September
Sow outdoors in mid July	*Dwarf: 'The Prince'*	mid September to mid October

laborious but gives much better results.

Space the plants 15 cm (6 inches) apart in each direction, or 5-8 cm (2-3 inches) apart in rows 30 cm (1 ft) apart. Take precautions against slugs in the early stages, keep the ground mulched to conserve moisture, and keep down weeds. Push small twigs between the plants to give some support and to help keep the pods off the ground.

The sowing plan opposite is recommended for a continous supply of French beans from June to October.

Pests and Diseases: Aphids are the most likely pest. Halo blight is a disease that causes brown spots on the leaves surrounded by a yellow 'halo'. Burn affected plants and grow your French beans on different ground next year.

Harvesting: Keep picking the beans regularly while still tender. This also encourages further cropping.

RUNNER BEANS*

Runner beans are a very popular, decorative and heavily yielding vegetable, many people preferring the flavour to that of French beans.

Most of the varieties are vigorous climbers, reaching up to 3 metres (10 ft). If dwarfer beans are required, grow the variety 'Kelvedon Marvel', nipping out the growing point when the plant starts to flower. Runner beans cannot stand frost and need a fairly long season, so they are unlikely to succeed in the coldest parts of the country. Good varieties are 'Achievement', 'Enorma', 'Prizewinner', 'Scarlet Emperor' and 'Streamline'.

Cultivation: Runner beans like really fertile soil. If possible prepare it the previous autumn by making a trench about one spade deep and 60 cm (2ft) wide. Put in a really thick layer of manure, and mix it in well with the soil from the trench. Choose a lightly sheltered position, say alongside a hedge. This encourages the insects necessary for pollination so that the beans will set (it is not true that syringeing the flowers helps them to set).

Sow the seeds outdoors in late May in the South, early June in the North. Sow 5 cm (2 inches) deep, about 15 cm (6 inches) apart, in double rows about 60 cm (2 ft) apart.

The beans must have really sturdy supports as the weight of the mature crop is enormous. Traditional supports were stout crossed poles at least 2 metres (7 ft) high, with a cross-member along the top. Ideally, use one pole for each plant, or allow intermediate plants to climb up strings.

Bamboo canes can also be used. These are often roped together at the top to make a 'wigwam'. Alternatively, supports can be made utilizing string, or patented supports incorporating nylon netting.

Keep the plants well mulched, and water as generally suggested for legumes (see page 38).

Pests and diseases: Blackfly, halo blight (see French beans – page 41), and anthracnose are possible problems. The latter causes sunken brown spots on pods and brown patches on leaves. Affected plants are best destroyed.

Runner beans, with their scarlet flowers, make an attractive climber

PEAS**

Ordinary garden peas are shelled and the green peas eaten. With the sugar or mange-tout peas, which are deservedly becoming increasingly popular, the whole pod is eaten while the peas are still immature. The dual-purpose mange-tout variety 'Sugar Snap' can be eaten early as pods, or allowed to mature and shelled for peas.

In seed catalogues peas are divided into 'earlies', 'second earlies', and 'maincrop' varieties, the difference between them being the time they take to mature. Earlies are ready in a minimum of 11 weeks, while maincrop varieties take up to 14 weeks. There are also round- and wrinkle-seeded types, the round being hardier and useful for very late and very early sowings, the wrinkle-seeded less hardy but sweeter and better flavoured. Peas vary in height from about 45 cm (1½ ft) to 1.5 metres (5 ft), the taller types being less convenient but heavier yielding.

Good first early varieties are 'Feltham First', 'Early Onward', 'Hurst Beagle', 'Kelvedon Wonder', 'Little Marvel', and 'Meteor'. Good second earlies are 'Hurst Green Shaft', 'Onward', and 'Victory Freezer', while recommended maincrop varieties are 'Senator' and 'Lord Chancellor'.

Cultivation: Peas need an open site and well-worked, well-manured soil. If possible prepare a trench the previous autumn as suggested for runner beans; otherwise dig plenty of manure into the ground several months before sowing. Peas like coolish weather,

Maturing crop of peas; regular picking promotes further cropping

so in mid summer they can be grown in light shade.

Like French beans, they will not germinate in cold soil. Early sowings should be made under cloches. Alternatively take out the drills and cover them with cloches to warm the soil, or simply expose them to the sun, for a few hours before sowing. Peas can also be sown indoors in pots or blocks as suggested for French beans.

There are several methods of sowing peas outdoors:–

1. Make a flat-bottomed drill about 23 cm (9 inches) wide and 4 cm (1½ inches) deep, spacing the seeds 5 cm (2 inches) apart.
2. Sow in bands of three rows, each row 12 cm (4½ inches) apart, the seeds also 12 cm (4½ inches) apart. Allow 45 cm (1½ ft) between the bands.
3. Sow in blocks or patches up to 90 cm (3 ft) wide, making the holes with the dibber about 4 cm (1½ inches) deep, spacing the seeds 5-8 cm (2-3 inches) apart.

Make the earliest sowings outdoors under cloches in late February or March in a sheltered position, using an early variety.

Make the main summer sowings from April until early July, using second early and maincrop varieties. It is also worth trying to get a late autumn crop by sowing an early variety in July. In good summers this will pay off.

In mild parts of the country hardy, overwintering peas can be sown in October and November to produce very early crops the following spring. Protect them with cloches in severe weather.

It is important to support the peas as soon as any tendrils are visible. Small twigs are adequate for dwarf varieties, but taller varieties need longer twigs or some kind of pea netting. Water and mulch peas, as suggested for legumes (see page 38)

Pests and Diseases: Mice can be a serious problem with early and late pea sowings. Set mousetraps fairly near the rows, protected with upturned tiles, or by placing them in pipes.

Birds also attack peas at all stages. Protect seedlings with black cotton (see page 23), and larger plants with netting.

Maggoty peas are caused by the pea moth. You can only take preventive measures such as spraying or dusting with derris a week after the plants start flowering. Early and late sowings often escape attack.

Harvesting: As with beans, pick regularly to encourage further cropping. Mange-tout peas are ready when the immature peas can just be seen as bumps inside the pod.

ROOT VEGETABLES

Of all vegetables, the roots are the most underrated. Many are very nutritious and have a superb flavour, which is only appreciated to the full when they are home-grown. In the hands of an imaginative cook excellent dishes can be made with root vegetables. Not only hot dishes; in a number of cases their flavour is brought out to the full if they are cooked, then eaten cold. This is true of beetroot, celeriac, kohl rabi, parsnip, hamburg parsley and even potatoes. Some are surprisingly good grated raw in salads – beetroot, carrots, celeriac, kohl rabi, turnips, and Jerusalem artichokes.

The root vegetables come into their own in the winter months; they can almost all be stored. Some of them can simply be left in the ground; others are less hardy or gradually deteriorate in the soil, so need to be lifted and stored under cover. As a rough guide, when roots are grown expressly for storage they should be sown on the late side, and grown relatively close together. This is rather contrary to expectations, but the purpose is to avoid over-sized and coarse vegetables, which do not store particularly well and have less flavour.

Overall root vegetables benefit from having plenty of organic matter in the soil, but try to avoid ultra fresh manure, whch makes the growth unhealthily lush. Rich, light soils are particularly suitable for roots, allowing them to expand easily and to produce nice clean roots.

Root vegetables require a steady supply of moisture but must not be overwatered, which encourages the development of leaves and shoots rather than of roots. Exceptions are potatoes, which require plenty of moisture if they are to yield heavily, and celeriac, which is a marsh plant by nature.

ARTICHOKES, JERUSALEM*

Jerusalem artichokes are tasty, nutritious tubers, which can be baked or boiled like potatoes, or used to make an excellent winter soup. They are easily grown, and one of the most suitable crops with which to break in heavy, previously uncultivated soil. They will, however, tolerate a wide range of soils.

The only problem with Jerusalem artichokes is that they are apt to spread unless efforts are made to keep them within bounds. They grow very tall, up to 3 metres (10 ft), so can usefully be planted two to three deep around the outside of a vegetable patch as a windbreak. Or you can use them to screen off an unsightly feature.

Tall Jerusalem artichoke plants

Jerusalem artichokes are useful for feeding domestic animals. The tubers can be cooked up for chickens, while rabbits and goats love the green foliage.

Cultivation: The knobbly tubers can be planted any time between February and May, about 10-15 cm (4-6 inches) deep and 30 cm (1 ft) apart. They are not always available in garden shops, but you can always buy a few from a greengrocer. Tubers the size of a hen's egg are said to be best, but larger tubers can be cut into several pieces, provided each has a shoot.

Once planted they require very little attention. In exposed gardens earth up the stems when the plants are about 30 cm (1 ft) high, so that they are not rocked by winds. Eventually they produce flowers like small sunflowers, but in mid summer cut the tops back to 1.5-1.8 metres (5-6 ft). This helps to direct energy into the formation of tubers, and also increases the stability of the plants. When the foliage dies off in autumn cut the stems back to a few inches from the ground.

Pests and diseases: Slugs may be a problem in some soils. Sclerotinia rot, which appears as a fluffy white mould at the base of the stems, is seen occasionally; affected plants are best destroyed.

Harvesting: The tubers are extremely hardy and can be left in the ground all winter and lifted as required. Always keep back a few tubers for planting the following year, but to prevent them spreading be sure you lift even the tiniest tubers and broken pieces.

Young summer beetroot pulled ready for use

BEETROOT*

Beetroot can be pulled fresh from the garden from about the end of May until late autumn, and then either pickled, or lifted and stored, for the winter. There are flat, round and long, tapered varieties in red, yellow and white forms.

Many varieties are liable to bolt (run to seed) rather than form roots if sown early in the year and/or subjected to spells of cold weather. Fortunately newer varieties such as 'Avonearly' and 'Boltardy' are 'bolt resistant' and suitable for these early sowings.

Cultivation: Beetroot needs rich, light soil. Very acid soils should be limed. If possible use ground manured for the previous crop.

The roots are best used when young and tender, before they become tough. So for a continuous supply of good quality beet it is advisable to make several sowings.

The first sowings can be made in March under cloches, followed by unprotected sowings outdoors in late March and April, in both cases using bolt-resistant varieties. Make further sowings at monthly intervals until July using any variety. For winter storage sow any of the round varities, or 'Cheltenham Greentop', one of the long varieties, in late May or June.

Beetroot should never be sown thickly, because the so-called seed is in fact a fruit containing several seeds, all of which may germinate. Single seeded, 'monogerm' beet is sometimes available, and if so, is worth using. Sow seed 1-1½ cm (½-¾ inch) deep, about

2.5 cm (1 inch) apart, thinning later to the required distance. Rather surprisingly early crops need the widest spacing. They can be as far apart as 8 cm (3 inches) between plants, in rows 20 cm (8 inches) apart. Main summer supplies and beet for winter storage can be 2.5 cm (1 inch) apart in rows 30 cm (1 ft) apart. Beet can also be sown indoors in soil or peat blocks and transplanted once the soil has warmed up.

Sparrows can be a problem in the seedling stage. Protect the plants with strands of black cotton (see page 23) or use wire netting.

Beet needs to grow steadily, so the aim with any watering should be to prevent the soil drying out. If possible you should water at the rate of 11 litres/sq metre (about 2 gallons/sq yd) every two to three weeks in a dry season. A top-dressing of a general fertilizer might be necessary during the growing season if growth is poor.

Pests and diseases: Blackfly can sometimes be troublesome. Beetroot are also affected by a leaf spot that disfigures the leaves – just pick off affected leaves, the root should be unaffected.

Harvesting: Summer beet are pulled as required. For winter storage lift the roots carefully in late autumn and twist off the stems. Store them in a frost-free place in layers, in boxes of moist peat or sand, or in clamps outdoors. If you are unable to provide any of these conditions, you can try using polythene sacks.

CARROTS**

Carrots are fussy about soil. They will always do far better on rich, light sandy soils, where the roots can expand without difficulty, than on heavy clay or stony soils. If you have heavy soil, work in as much organic matter as possible to improve it.

There are several different types of carrots. For early crops use the smaller finger-shaped carrots of the Amsterdam and Nantes types (good varieties are 'Amsterdam Colora' and 'Nantes Express'), or the little round carrots such as 'Early French Frame' and the selection 'Early French Frame – Rondo'.

For the main summer supply and winter storage use the larger Chantenay, Berlicum or Autumn King types. Good varieties are 'Chantenay Red Cored', 'Berlicum-Berjo', and 'Autumn King-Vita Longa'.

Cultivation: For a continuous supply several sowings have to be made. Provided the soil is warm enough (carrots need a minimum soil temperature of 7°C (45°F) to germinate), make the first sowings in frames or under cloches in late February or in March. Follow this with unprotected outdoor sowings in March or April. For both these sowings use early varieties; they will be ready in June and July.

For later summer use and winter storage, sow maincrop varieties from May until mid July at roughly four-week intervals. Finally, for a very late crop of small roots in November and December, sow an early variety in August, covering them with cloches in September or October.

Carrots should be sown very thinly (to minimize thin-

Fine crop of early carrots pulled ready for use

ning), about 1 cm (½ inch) deep. The highest yields are obtained by growing them in rows about 15 cm (6 inches) apart. Early carrots, which should be encouraged to grow very fast, can be thinned to 8-10 cm (3-4 inches) apart. Maincrop carrots can be thinned to 3.5 cm (1½ inches) apart. Weed between the rows in the early stages; subsequently the natural canopy of leaves will help to prevent further weed growth.

Carrots will not grow well if the soil is allowed to dry out, and the roots are likely to split if there is heavy rain, or heavy watering, after a dry spell. Watering at the rate of about 22 litres/sq metre (3-4 gallons/sq yd), every two to three weeks will usually ensure steady growth.

Pests and diseases: Carrot fly is an almost universal problem with carrots, causing very poor crops. The flies are attracted by the smell of carrot foliage, and lay eggs which hatch into tiny grubs visible on the roots. There are no completely effective and harmless chemical remedies, but the following measures can be taken to minimize attacks where the problem is serious.

Concentrate on early sowings (February and March), and on late sowings (June and July), which escape the worst attacks.

Sow very thinly, and thin on calm, still evenings, nipping off surplus seedlings rather than pulling them out. Remove and burn the thinnings, or bury them deep in the compost heap (this all helps to put the flies off the scent).

Celeriac, grown in a reasonably open sunny position

Grow carrots in raised beds about 15 cm (6 inches) high, or in boxes, or under cloches, or in beds surrounded by wooden boards. These measures deter the flies because they only fly low.

Use the less leafy varieties such as the Amsterdam and Nantes types.

Lift maincrop varieties by October to prevent the late brood hatching.

Incidentally there is some hope for the future: plant breeders are now working on producing varieties which are resistant to carrot fly!

Harvesting: Pull the carrots during the summer months as required. In mild areas on well drained soils, carrots can be left in the ground in winter, covered with about 30 cm (1 ft) of leaves or straw. Otherwise lift them carefully in autumn and twist off the stems. Store them in layers, in boxes of moist peat or sand, in a frost-free place.

CELERIAC**

Celeriac is a member of the celery family and forms a large, rather knobbly swollen bulb at the base of the stem. Although a little tricky to scrub clean, this makes an excellent winter vegetable. It can be boiled and served with a cheese sauce, or used in soup, or grated raw in salads. The leaves have a strong celery flavour and can be used, sparingly, as a celery substitute.

Purple variety of kohl rabi – one of the most unusual root vegetables

Cultivation: Celeriac, being a marshland plant, must have fertile, moisture-retentive soil, rich in organic matter. It also needs a long growing season if it is to reach a reasonable size. It is best sown indoors, in gentle heat, in February or March. Germination is often erratic, but once seedlings have germinated, prick them out and harden them off, ready for planting in the open in late April, May or June.

Plant about 35 cm (14 inches) apart each way, taking care not to bury the crowns. The key to success is plenty of moisture. So water generously in dry weather, and keep the ground between the plants mulched to conserve moisture. Celeriac responds well to feeding with a seaweed-based fertilizer during the growing season. Towards the end of July the outer leaves can be removed, which exposes the crowns and is said to encourage them to swell.

Pests and diseases: Celeriac is unlikely to be troubled by many pests, but leaf miners can tunnel and blister the leaves. Remove and destroy affected leaves.

Harvesting: The crowns are ready for use from about October onwards. They are very hardy so can be left in the soil all winter. However, tuck a thick layer of straw or bracken between the plants to protect them from frost, and to make it easier to dig them out when the ground is frozen. They will normally remain in good condition until April or May, when they will run to seed.

KOHL RABI*

Kohl rabi is an extraordinary looking vegetable. A swollen ball forms on the stem, which appears to be suspended a couple of inches above the ground. Provided it is used young, kohl rabi has an unusual, delicate flavour, which is much appreciated on the Continent, where it is more widely grown.

Being one of the brassicas, it should be rotated with them in the garden. It tolerates dry conditions well, so is sometimes grown as a substitute for turnips, which do poorly in dry soils. It does best in fertile, light, sandy soil, and is fast growing, being ready six to ten weeks after sowing.

There are green- and purple-skinned forms of kohl rabi. As a general rule the more tender green varieties are sown until about June, and the somewhat tougher purple varieties in July and August.

Cultivation: Kohl rabi can be sown in succession from late February, in mild areas, until August. Either sow in seed trays and plant out when the seedlings are no more than 5 cm (2 inches) tall, or sow thinly in rows 30 cm (1 ft) apart, thinning as early as possible to about 23 cm (9 inches) between plants.

Pests and diseases: Seedlings may sometimes be attacked by flea beetle.

Harvesting: Use kohl rabi when it is between golf ball and tennis ball size: once they are larger they become tough and flavourless. Cook them without peeling, as much of the flavour lies just below the skin. They are excellent stuffed like green peppers.

HAMBURG PARSLEY*

Hamburg parsley is a dual-purpose winter vegetable, with fine-flavoured, parsnip-like roots, and foliage very much like that of broad leaved parsley. It is hardy, so the roots can be lifted from the ground all winter while the leaves, which unlike ordinary parsley remain green even in fairly severe weather, serve as a useful parsley substitute. This vegetable is easier to grow than parsnips, liking reasonably fertile, but not freshly manured soil. It grows quite successfully in light shade.

Cultivation: Hamburg parsley needs a long growing season, so sow outside in March (once the soil has warmed up), April, or early May. Sow ½-1 cm (¼-½ inch) deep, in drills 30 cm (1 ft) apart, thinning early to about 23 cm (9 inches) apart. It can also be sown indoors in February or early March, preferably in soil or peat blocks or small pots. Transplant the seedlings outdoors, after hardening off, when they are no more than 5 cm (2 inches) high. Keep the plants weeded, and water to prevent the soil drying out.

Pests and diseases: These are unlikely to be a problem.

Harvesting: The roots are ready by late October. They can be left in the soil, although there is some risk of slug damage, especially on heavy soils. Otherwise lift them, trim off the leaves, and store them in a frost-free shed, in layers in boxes of moist peat or sand. To cook, it is best simply to wash and scrub the roots as they discolour when peeled, and some of the flavour is lost.

PARSNIPS*

Parsnips roasted around the Sunday joint are one of the treats of winter. Like so many root crops, they do best on deep, light, rich, stone-free soil, rather than on heavy soil. Improve the soil by working in plenty of well-rotted organic manure beforehand. It has always been suggested that manure causes parsnip roots to fork, but research has indicated that this is not so.

Cultivation: Grow parsnips in an open position. They need a long growing season, but will not germinate in cold soil. Sow outside from early March (provided the soil has warmed up) until early May. Only sow new seed, as parsnip seed loses its viability very rapidly. Sow the large, flat seeds 1-2 cm (½-¾ inch) deep, in rows about 25 cm (10 inches) apart. To minimize thinning sow two or three seeds in groups at 'stations' 13 cm (5 inches) apart, thinning to one per station once the seedlings start to show. Germination is often slow, so it is a good idea to sow a few radish seeds between the stations to mark the rows.

Parsnips can also be started off indoors. Sow seed in soil or peat blocks or small pots in February or early March.

Parsnips – these are best pulled from the ground as required

Transplant the seedlings outdoors, after hardening off, when they are no more than 5 cm (2 inches) high.

Keep the plants weeded, and water in dry weather at the rates suggested for beetroot (see page 46).

Pests and diseases: Perhaps the most serious disease of parsnips is canker, especially on rich, organic soils. The tops of the roots blacken and crack, and eventually rot. If this is a problem on your soil, grow canker resistant 'White Gem' and 'Avonresister' varieties.

Harvesting: The roots are ready from October onwards, and should be left in the soil until required, just pulling a little soil over the crowns to protect them. In low temperatures some of the starch in the roots is converted into sugar, making them sweeter. The foliage dies down completely so mark the end of the rows with sticks so that they can be found in snow.

POTATOES*

Potatoes take up a lot of space and are relatively cheap to buy, so if your garden is small, it is probably only worth growing 'earlies', which are so superb when dug straight from the ground and are ready when shop prices are still high. They also escape some of the pests and diseases that affect maincrop potatoes.

Potatoes should always be rotated over at least a three-year cycle to avoid the build up of soil pests and diseases, especially eelworm.

There are a confusing number of potato varieties to choose from, all with different characteristics. The following are particularly good:

Earlies: 'Maris Bard', 'Suttons Foremost'.

Second earlies: these take a little longer to mature – 'Red Craig's Royal', 'Wilja'.

Maincrop: these take longest to mature but give the heaviest yields – 'Desiree', 'King Edward', 'Pentland Squire'.

Potatoes need deeply dug, fertile soil with plenty of manure or compost in it, a good supply of nitrogen, and most important of all, plenty of moisture throughout growth. They will tolerate fairly acid soil.

Cultivation: Buy seed potatoes in February and start them into growth by 'chitting' or sprouting them. Stand them upright (the eyes uppermost), in shallow boxes or trays (egg trays are ideal) in a cool room on a north-facing windowsill. Within about six weeks the potatoes will sprout: when the shoots are about 2 cm (¾ inch) long they can be planted, provided the soil and weather permit.

Earlies can be planted outdoors from about mid March onwards, followed by second earlies and maincrops in April and May. Make a drill or individual holes 10-13 cm (4-5 inches) deep, and plant the tubers upright. Both earlies and second earlies should be planted about 38 cm (15 inches) apart in rows 38-45 cm (15-18 inches) apart; maincrop potatoes should be spaced the same distance apart in rows 75 cm (2½ ft) apart.

Early potatoes may need protection from frost. Either cover the leaves with newspaper if frost is forecast, or draw the earth up around the young growths.

Potatoes – harvest carefully to avoid damaged tubers

As the plants grow, tubers near the surface are pushed upwards and become greened – and therefore harmful. To prevent this the plants should be earthed up when they are about 23 cm (9 inches) high. Pull earth up around the stems to a height of about 10-13 cm (4-5 inches).

Potatoes are sometimes grown under black plastic film, to cut down weeding and avoid earthing up. If you try this, plant the tubers shallowly and anchor the plastic over them afterwards. When the leaves bulge up beneath the

plastic cut a slit and pull them through. Harvest the tubers by rolling back the plastic: they will be found virtually on the surface of the soil.

Potatoes are heavy feeders and drinkers. Unless the soil is very fertile, work a general fertilizer into the soil before planting, and give a nitrogenous top-dressing, or a liquid feed with a seaweed-based fertilizer, during the growing season.

In dry weather the yields of early potatoes will be increased by watering roughly every fortnight at the rate of 16-22 litres/sq metre (3-4 gallons/sq yd). With maincrop potatoes the critical point is when the potatoes are the size of marbles. Give them one, very heavy watering at 22-27 litres/sq metre (4-5 gallons/sq yd) at this stage.

Pests and diseases: In humid areas maincrop potatoes are often affected by blight, causing brown patches on the leaves. Prevent this by spraying with a copper-based fungicide in early July. In late August the haulm of affected potatoes can be cut back to within a few inches of the ground to prevent blight spreading to the tubers.

Eelworm causes weak and stunted plants, the lower leaves withering and the upper ones wilting during the day. Small tubers and pinhead cysts on the roots are a fairly sure indication of the problem, which is caused by microscopic pests. The only practical remedy for amateurs if the ground is infected is rotation. Where eelworm is a problem, grow the new varieties that have resistance to the commonest types of eelworm; these include 'Pentland Javelin', 'Pentland Lustre', 'Pentland Meteor' and 'Maris Piper' (maincrop).

Harvesting: Lift early potatoes as required. Maincrop potatoes can be lifted for storage once the leaves have died down. Choose a warm day, spread them on the ground for an hour or so to dry, then store them in hessian sacks, or double-thickness paper sacks, in a frost-free room or shed. They must be kept dark. Cover the sacks with extra matting or blankets if freezing conditions are expected.

SALSIFY AND SCORZONERA*

These two roots are always linked together, though salsify is a biennial, running to seed in its second year, and scorzonera is a perennial. They are normally grown for their long, tapered, well-flavoured roots. It is less well known that their flowering buds, which have a delicious asparagus flavour, are also edible, as are the open flowers which can be used in salads or even pickled!

Cultivation: If you are growing salsify or scorzonera for their roots it is almost essential to have a deep light soil: they rarely develop roots of substantial dimensions on very heavy or stony soils. Sow fresh seed – as with parsnip seed,

Long, thin tapered roots of scorzonera

viability is lost after one season. From March to May sow seed 2 cm (¾ inch) deep, in rows about 20 cm (8 inches) apart, thinning to about 10 cm (4 inches) apart. Germination is sometimes erratic, so use radishes to mark the rows as suggested for parsnips.

Pests and diseases: Both salsify and scorzonera are usually trouble-free.

Harvesting: The roots are ready in October and can be lifted as required. If the scorzonera are no more than pencil thin, leave them in the ground for another year to thicken up. The roots of both are hardy and can be left in the soil all winter, though some protection with straw or bracken is advisable.

If the flower buds are wanted, leave the plants in the soil and they will flower the following spring. The flower buds are picked with 8-10 cm (3-4 inch) stems, just before the flowers open. Cook them like asparagus.

SWEDES*

The large, rounded, usually yellow-fleshed roots of swedes are extremely hardy, very sweet flavoured, and invaluable for winter. They belong to the brassica family, and therefore should be carefully rotated in the garden with the other brassicas.

Swedes do badly in very dry and very wet soils. They require light, fertile soil, limed if acid, and preferably manured for a previous crop.

Cultivation: It is only necessary to make one sowing of swedes, in late April or early May in the North, or late May and early June in the South. Sow seed 2 cm (¾ inch) deep, in rows 38-45 cm (15-18 inches) apart, thinning as early as possible to about 25 cm (10 inches) apart.

In dry weather water enough to prevent the soil drying out; but don't overwater, otherwise much of the flavour will be lost.

Pests and diseases: Watch out for flea beetle attacks at the seedling stage. Mildew, which looks like a white powder on the leaves, and clubroot, can be real problems. If you've had these troubles, try the excellent new variety 'Marian', which has considerable resistance to both diseases and is well worth growing.

Harvesting: Roots can be ready from September onwards in the South, October onwards in the North. Leave them in the ground until Christmas, when they should be lifted before they become woody. They can be stored in clamps outdoors, or layered in boxes of moist peat or sand and kept in a frost-free place.

TURNIPS*

Provided the soil is reasonably fertile and there is plenty of moisture, turnips are among the fastest-maturing vegetables. They can be used fresh in spring and summer, or stored for winter use. When the plants are grown close together, leafy turnip tops can be used as greens, which are very useful in spring.

The white-fleshed turnips are grown for summer use and should be pulled young and small, no more than 5 cm (2 inches) across. Good varieties are 'Purple Top Milan' and 'Snowball'. The yellow-fleshed varieties, such as 'Golden Ball' and 'Manchester Market' ('Green Top Stone') are hardier, slower-maturing, and best for winter use.

Turnips are brassicas, so should be rotated accordingly. They prefer ground that has been manured for a previous crop; if the soil is not very fertile, work in a general fertilizer before sowing.

Cultivation: For summer turnips make the first sowings under cloches in March, followed by sowings at monthly intervals until July, when the winter crop can be sown. The mid summer sowings can be made in light shade, as turnips dislike intense heat.

Sow the seed about 2 cm (¾ inch) deep, the summer crop in rows 23 cm (9 inches) apart, and thin to 10 cm (4 inches) apart; the winter crop in rows 30 cm (1 ft) apart, and thin to 15 cm (6 inches) apart. As turnips grow so fast it is important to thin as soon as the seedlings touch one another.

For turnip tops, sow winter varieties either in August or September, or summer varieties in early spring, as soon as the soil has warmed up. Either sow a small broadcast patch, or sow thinly in rows 15 cm (6 inches) apart, leaving them unthinned.

Pests and diseases: Flea beetle attacks can be a problem at the seedling stage. On ground infested with clubroot, turnips may be affected (see page 25).

Harvesting: Pull summer turnips from the end of May onwards. Lift winter turnips around Christmas and twist off the stems. Store them in a frost-free place, layered in boxes of moist peat or sand, or in clamps outdoors.

Turnip tops are cut 2.5 cm (1 inch) above ground level when the plants are about 15 cm (6 inches) high. The plants often re-sprout, so two or three cuts can be made.

White-fleshed turnips, pulled young and small

THE ONION FAMILY

Cooking without onions is rather like swimming without water: every kitchen garden worth the name should devote some space to one or two members of the onion family. Almost all of them require fertile, well-worked, and above all well-drained soil, ideally with well-rotted manure worked in for the previous crop. Acid soils should be limed.

In spite of the 'onion bed' tradition, onions should be rotated on at least a three-year cycle to avoid the build up of soil-borne pests and diseases in the ground.

With their narrow leaves onions rarely form a weed-smothering canopy over the soil, so it is important to keep them weed-free from the early stages onwards.

GARLIC**

Probably because of its associations with the Mediterranean, it is often assumed that garlic is difficult to grow here. That's not so: it is very hardy and can be grown most successfully, though it certainly does very much better on light, well-drained soils than on heavy soils. If your soil is heavy, work sand or ashes into the bottom of the drill before planting, or plant the garlic on a slight ridge to improve the drainage.

Cultivation: Wherever possible, plant garlic in the autumn, from September to November; otherwise plant in February or March, as soon as the soil is workable. Plant single cloves from a bulb about 4 cm (1½ inches) deep, so that the tips just protrude above soil level. Space them about 10 cm (4 inches) apart in rows 15 cm (6 inches) apart. Other than keeping them weed-free, little further attention is required.

Pests and diseases: Garlic is usually trouble-free.

Harvesting: The bulbs can be lifted for storage once the foliage has died down naturally. Lift them very carefully as they bruise easily, then dry them off in the sun outdoors or in a greenhouse until they are blanched white. Plait them into ropes, or hang them in nets, in a cool, dry, frost-free place for use throughout the winter. They may keep for up to 10 months.

LEEKS*

The leek season can be spread from September to early May by selecting appropriate varieties. Early varieties are long with pale foliage, while the later, hardier varieties are stockier and darker-leaved. Recommended varieties are:

Earlies: 'Autumn Mammoth-Walton Mammoth'.

Mid season: 'Autumn Mammoth-Argenta'.

Late: 'Autumn Mammoth-Herwina', and 'Giant Winter-Catalina'.

Because leeks belong to the onion family they should be rotated with onions. They require an open position and rich, well-prepared soil, with plenty of organic matter worked into it. This can be done shortly before planting. They also have a high nitrogen requirement, so apply a nitrogenous fertilizer before planting, or feed with a seaweed-based fertilizer during growth.

Cultivation: Leeks need a long growing season. The first sowings can be made indoors in gentle heat in February for planting out, after hardening off, in May. Make the first outdoor sowings in a seed-bed or under cloches from March (provided the soil has warmed up) to May. Sow in drills 2 cm (¾ inch) deep.

The main plantings are made in June, continuing into July and early August. The ideal size for transplanting is about 20 cm (8 inches) tall; the larger the seedling, the sooner it will mature, so plant in order of size along a row to make lifting convenient.

Water the seed-bed thoroughly before lifting the seedlings, and trim off the tips of the leaves to prevent them dragging on the soil. Then make holes about 15 cm (6 inches) deep with the dibber and drop the leek into the hole. The earth will fall back in naturally, so blanching the stem. Leeks can also be planted in a V-shaped drill about 8 cm (3 inches) deep. Fill in the drill as the plants grow to blanch the stem. The rows can be 25-30 cm (10-12 inches) apart, spacing the leeks 15 cm (6 inches) apart, or closer if you

want smaller leeks, which some people prefer.

Make sure the ground is moist after planting, watering daily (about a cupful for each plant) if necessary. Except in very dry weather no further watering is required unless you want very large leeks.

Pests and diseases: Leeks are unlikely to be troubled by

Leeks planted in rows; they are ready for lifting in autumn

serious pests or diseases, although downy mildew can be an occasional problem in cool, damp seasons.

Harvesting: Lift leeks as required during autumn and winter, starting with the earlier varieties.

ONIONS*

There are two main types of onion – bulb onions and salad onions. With bulb onions the large, swollen bulbs are used fresh, or stored for winter. With spring or salad onions, the young green leaf and shank, and sometimes the slightly swollen little white bulbs, are eaten – in salads or chopped for flavouring.

Bulb onions: These need a long growing season, and are either raised from sets, which are specially prepared miniature bulbs, or from seed. Sets give them a head start in life and are easier to grow, especially in poorer soils, but they have a tendency to bolt, and only certain varieties are available, for example 'Ailsa Craig', 'Sturon' and 'Stuttgarter Giant', the last two being good keepers. Seed, although a little trickier to grow, works out cheaper and offers a far greater choice of variety. Here recommended modern varieties are 'Rijnsburger Wijbo', and for storing 'Rijnsburger Balstora' and 'Hygro'. Good Japanese varieties for autumn sowing are 'Express Yellow', 'Imai Early Yellow' and 'Senshyu Semi-Globe Yellow'. 'Brunswick Blood Red' is a good red onion variety to choose.

Cultivation: Sets are planted from February until April. Select small rather than large sets as they are less likely to bolt. Sets that have been 'heat treated' to discourage bolting are sometimes available: these should not be planted until late March or April.

Make drills about 2.5 cm (1 inch) deep, and plant the sets so that their tips just appear above ground. They can be from 5-10 cm (2-4 inches) apart, the wider spacing giving larger bulbs, in rows about 23 cm (9 inches) apart. Birds sometimes tweak out the sets: if so dig them out completely and replant, rather than pushing them back in. The rows can be protected with black cotton (see page 23).

When using seed, prepare a seed-bed with a finely raked surface about 10 days before sowing to allow it to 'settle'. This discourages the onion fly, which lays its eggs on freshly disturbed soil, and causes seedlings to wilt and die, especially under dry conditions.

For a continuous year-round supply, two sowings should be made, the first with standard varieties from February to April, starting as soon as soil conditions allow. They can also be started indoors in gentle heat in January or February and planted out in March. These will mature in August and September, and the best 'keepers' will last until the following April.

For supplies in the gap that follows in June and July use the Japanese varieties. Sow them in early August in the North of the British Isles, in mid August in the Midlands, and the end of August in the South. Although these cannot be stored for long, they are hardier and more reliable than the old autumn-sown varieties.

Sow onions very thinly about 1 cm (½ inch) deep, in rows about 25 cm (10 inches) apart. They should be thinned in stages, starting as early as possible, until they are 4-10 cm (1½-4 inches) apart, the wider spacing producing the largest onions. Use the thinnings as spring onions.

Bulb onions – one of the most widely grown vegetables

Spring onions: For a regular supply of these, start sowing under cloches in February, and continue sowing at roughly fortnightly intervals until June, using the variety 'White Lisbon'. For very early supplies the following year sow 'White Lisbon-Winter Hardy' in July in the North, August in the South. Prepare seed-bed as for other onions but sow thinly, and 'thin' simply by pulling as required.

Pickling onions: Good varieties are 'Paris Silver Skin', 'Barletta' and 'The Queen'. Sow the seed less than 2 cm (¾ inch) apart in rows 25 cm (10 inches) apart or in bands about 23 cm (9 inches) wide. No thinning is required as the competition will keep the bulbs small. They will succeed in poorer soils than bulb onions.

Pests and diseases: Onion fly is the most likely pest. The yellowing leaves droop and maggots will be found at the base of the bulb. Destroy affected plants. As a precaution, bromophos can be raked into the soil before sowing or planting.

Harvesting: Onions to use fresh are pulled as required during the season. Onions for storage and pickling are lifted once the foliage has died back naturally. Don't bend them over, as this increases the chances of the onions sprouting in store. Bulbs for storage should be lifted and handled gently, and if possible dried off in the sun and wind outdoors, off the ground on upturned boxes. Dry them indoors if it is very wet. Store them for winter in a dry, frost-free place, either plaited in ropes or hung in nets. Never store thick-necked or diseased bulbs.

Shallots suspended above the ground on a wire frame to dry

SHALLOTS*

Shallots are a chunky-shaped type of onion, very much prized for pickling. They also make an excellent substitute for onions in early summer, as they keep better than any other onions, remaining in good condition until June. Single sets can multiply into clumps of up to 20 bulbs. There are both red- and yellow-skinned varieties – both equally good!

Cultivation: Buy small, good quality, virus-free sets: the ideal size is 2 cm (¾ inch) diameter (larger sets may 'bolt'). They can be planted in December or January in mild areas on well-drained soil, but elsewhere plant them as early in the year as soil conditions permit. Plant them like onion sets 15 cm (6 inches) apart, in rows 25 cm (10 inches) apart.

Pests and diseases: Shallots are usually trouble-free.

Harvesting: Lift, dry and store as suggested for onions (see opposite). Provided the stock remains healthy, keep back a few of your own bulbs for planting the following year, though it is probably wise to start afresh with bought sets every three years.

SALAD VEGETABLES

Few vegetables are as rewarding to grow in terms of freshness and variety as salads. Today the marked revival of interest in salads is reflected by the greater variety of salad seed available. We tend to think of salads only as summer crops, but there are quite a number which are hardy, and can be picked from the garden all year round.

Many of these winter salads – corn salad, land cress, Mediterranean rocket and some of the endives and chicories – can be grown outdoors, but their quality and yield is always improved if they can be protected by cloches or low polythene tunnels. They can also be grown in unheated greenhouses, making good use of space which is often idle in the winter months.

The 'cut and come again' seedling crops, such as cress, mustard or rape, Mediterranean rocket and even lettuce, are invaluable for very small gardens. Miniature patches, no more than a couple of feet square, can be broadcast several times a year. Provided the ground is reasonably fertile and moist, several successive cuttings can be made when the seedlings are only a few inches high.

All leafy crops require fertile soil, with plenty of nitrogen and moisture throughout their growth. They rarely do well on dry or infertile soils. Exceptionally attractive salads can be made by blending together different salad plants. For the finishing touch, sprinkle borage or other finely chopped herbs over the top.

CELERY**

There are two types of celery. The traditional blanched, trench celery produces long, crunchy, white or coloured stalks between October and February. The more recently introduced 'self-blanching' types have shorter, greenish stems, which nevertheless have a good flavour. They are not hardy, but are ready between mid July and October. They are easier to grow and require less space than traditional celery, which demands time, space and skill.

Good varieties of trench celery are 'Giant Pink', 'Giant White' and 'Giant Red' (reflecting the stalk colour); reliable self-blanching varieties are 'Golden Self Blanching' and 'Lothom Self Blanching'. All of these are good both raw and cooked.

Cultivation: Celery requires moisture-retentive but well-drained, rich soil, with plenty of organic matter dug in beforehand. Very acid soils should be limed. For trench celery prepare a trench the previous autumn if possible. Dig it 30 cm (1 ft) deep, and about 38 cm (15 inches) wide for a single row, 50 cm (20 inches) wide for a double row. Work a thick layer of well-rotted manure into the trench, then replace the bulk of the removed soil to within 10 cm (4 inches) of the top.

Celery has a high nitrogen requirement, so a nitrogenous fertilizer can be applied before planting and during growth; use a seaweed-based fertilizer during growth.

Self-blanching celery grown in blocks of short rows

Sow seed in gentle heat indoors in late March or early April. Do not sow any earlier, as the seedlings may bolt (run to seed) if subjected to a cold spell, or indeed any 'shocks'. For this reason it is worth sowing in soil, or peat blocks or small pots, thinning to one seedling in each block. Sow on the surface without covering, as the seed requires light to germinate.

Plant out in late May or early June after hardening off. Plant trench celery in single rows 23 cm (9 inches) apart, or in staggered double rows 25 cm (10 inches) apart. Plant self-blanching celery in block formation about 23 cm (9 inches) apart each way.

In dry weather when celery is growing, water it heavily at a weekly rate of up to 22 litres/sq metre (4 gallons/sq yd).

Trench celery is earthed up in three stages, starting when the plants are about 30 cm (1 ft) high and repeating at three-weekly intervals until only the tips are visible. First tie the stems together just below the leaves, then pull earth up around the stalks to a depth of about 8 cm (3 inches). Trench celery can also be grown on the flat and blanched by tying dark paper or black polythene around the stems.

Pests and diseases: Slugs and celery fly are the worst pests. Take measures against slugs, and pick off leaves blistered by the celery fly, by hand.

Harvesting: Cut the stems at ground level when required. Self-blanching celery is destroyed by frost. Trench celery may need protection with straw during the winter to keep it in good condition.

CHICORY, WITLOOF**

Witloof or Belgian chicory is becoming increasingly popular; the bud-like, pale chicons make a pleasant winter salad and an equally good cooked vegetable. They are not difficult to grow, although the roots have to be forced in the dark to obtain the chicons. Very tight heads are be obtained with the new varieties 'Crispa' and 'Normato'.

Cultivation: Chicory requires reasonably fertile, but not freshly manured soil, in an open position. Sow the seed thinly outdoors in May or early June in rows 30 cm (1 ft) apart. Thin in stages to 15 cm (6 inches) apart. The plants look like large dandelions. Keep them weeded but otherwise leave until the autumn.

In late October or November dig up the roots and cut off the leaves about 2.5 cm (1 inch) above the crown. Reject any roots that are very fanged or very thin. To keep a household supplied throughout the winter it is best to force a few roots at a time, say every fortnight. Store the bulk of the roots until required for forcing in layers in a box of moist peat or sand, in an outdoor shed.

All that is required for forcing is complete darkness and a little warmth. A simple method is to pot up three roots, closely together, in any soil in a 23 cm (9 inch) plant pot. Cover this with an upturned pot of the same size, with aluminium foil over the drainage holes to exclude the light. Keep at a temperature of about 10°C (50°F) or a little higher. Provided the soil does not dry out, the chicons will develop in about three weeks.

Chicory roots can also be forced by planting them in greenhouse soil, and excluding light. This can be done by covering them with black polythene stretched over wire hoops, and anchored into the soil on either side.

Pests and diseases: Problems are unlikely.

Harvesting: Once the chicons are ready keep them in the dark until they are used, as they become green and bitter on exposure to light. Cut them about 2.5 cm (1 inch) above the crown. If left in the pot or ground they often re-sprout to yield a second, smaller crop.

CORN SALAD*

Corn salad or lamb's lettuce is a mild-flavoured salad plant grown mainly for use in autumn, winter and spring. It takes little space and is not fussy about soil or situation.

Cultivation: For the autumn to spring supply, sow it outdoors from June until early August. If the soil is dry at the time water the drill first, then sow the seed, and cover the seed with dry soil. This prevents evaporation and ensures germination. Sow in rows about 25 cm (10 inches) apart, and thin to 10 cm (4 inches) apart. In late autumn protect the plants with cloches if available, or with bracken or light straw, to keep them in better condition. Corn salad can also be sown outdoors in March or April for a summer supply.

Pests and diseases: These are not normally a problem, though aphids can sometimes attack.

Harvesting: Pick the leaves as required, leaving the plants in the ground. Leaves will continue to be produced over a period of several weeks.

CRESS, MUSTARD AND RAPE*

Mustard and cress are traditionally grown on blotting paper indoors, but are also useful and very productive salad crops when grown in an unheated greenhouse or in the open ground, particularly in early spring and autumn. Rape, which has a milder flavour than mustard, is often used commercially as a mustard substitute. It makes an excellent salad crop, and if allowed to grow taller, can be cooked and used as 'greens'.

Cultivation: Very small patches, say 30-60 cm (1-2 ft) square, of these seedling crops will provide large quantities of salad material over several weeks. Sowings can be made in February and March, and again in October, in unheated greenhouses, frames, or under cloches. The October sowings will provide pickings late in the year and again the following spring.

Sow outdoors from March to early May, and in September. Mid summer sowings may

Witloof or Belgian chicory – a crisp winter salad vegetable

Mild-flavoured corn salad – another useful winter crop

succeed, but are likely to run to seed rapidly in hot weather.

Prepare the soil, broadcast the seeds on the surface and cover with newspaper or plastic film to keep the soil moist until the seeds germinate.

Pests and diseases: Usually trouble-free, although 'damping off' may occur.

Harvesting: Start cutting the seedlings 1 cm (½ inch) above soil level when they are 5-8 cm (2-3 inches) high. If allowed to grow too high they can become very hot flavoured. If the patch is kept watered it will re-sprout, giving up to five cuts in cool weather, two or three in hot weather.

CUCUMBERS**

There are two types of cucumber. The best quality are the greenhouse or frame cucumbers, which are long and smooth. The plants climb to considerable heights, and require warm, humid conditions and careful attention. Much more rugged are the outdoor 'ridge' cucumbers. These are generally short and have prickly skins, though the improved Japanese varieties, such as 'Burpless Tasty Green' and 'Burpee Hybrid' are longer and smoother. 'Perfection' is one of the best of the old ridge varieties. Good greenhouse varieties are 'Telegraph Improved', 'Butcher's Disease Resisting', and the all-female variety 'Femspot'.

Gherkins are grown in exactly the same way as outdoor 'ridge' cucumbers. Suitable varieties for gherkins are 'Venlo' and 'Condor'.

Cultivation: Cucumber roots need to romp through strawy organic matter. Prepare the ground beforehand by making a trench, or digging individual holes, about 30 cm (1 ft) deep and the same width, filling them with well-rotted strawy manure, covered with about 15 cm (6 inches) of soil.

Cucumber plants dislike transplanting, so they should either be sown *in situ*, or in individual pots or soil or peat blocks to minimize the shock.

Outdoor cucumbers, which sprawl rather than climb, can either be grown on the flat, spaced about 60-75 cm (2-2½ ft) apart, or trained up trellises or supports spaced about 45 cm (1½ ft) apart. Sow them in mid May in the South, the end of May in the North. Sow two or three seeds together about 2 cm (¾ inch) deep, on their side, and cover with a jam-jar to assist germination. They can also be sown indoors in mid April, hardening off before planting out. Cloche protection in the early stages is beneficial.

To encourage fruiting the old types of ridge cucumber are 'stopped' (the growing point nipped out), above the fifth leaf. The strongest two or three laterals are then selected and also stopped beyond the fifth leaf, others being removed. The Japanese varieties bear fruit on the main stem and only need to be stopped when they reach the top of the support.

Outdoor ridge cucumbers

Keep the cucumbers well watered and mulched, and feed occasionally with a general fertilizer during growth.

Sow greenhouse or frame cucumbers in February, March or April in a propagator at soil temperatures of at least 20°C (68°F). For early crops the greenhouse or frame must be heated, with night temperatures of at least 16°C (60°F).

Plant 45 cm (1½ ft) apart, when the soil temperature reaches at least 16°C (60°F) and only in warm conditions; keep the greenhouse well ventilated in hot weather, but close it as soon as the temperature drops in the evening.

Cucumbers need to be tied to horizontal wire supports. Train them to the top of the wire then nip out the growing point; stop the laterals two leaves beyond a fruit.

With the older varieties it is necessary to remove the male flowers, as pollinated fruit is swollen and bitter. The female flowers are distinguished by a miniature cucumber visible behind the flower. With more recent 'all female' varieties this is no longer necessary.

Pests and diseases: Red spider mites can be a problem; keeping the greenhouse atmosphere moist by syringeing daily with water in hot weather will help to control them. Greenhouse cucumbers are subject to a number of diseases, so use disease-resistant varieties where possible.

Harvesting: Pick regularly to encourage further cropping. Cucumbers are mature when the ends are parallel, rather than pointed.

ENDIVE*

Although not widely grown here, endives are very useful salad plants all the year round, but especially in autumn, winter and spring. They are slightly bitter compared to lettuce, but this can be remedied by partial or complete blanching, or by shredding them fairly finely in salads. There are two distinct types: the broad-leaved or Batavian, and the curly-leaved, which has finely divided, attractive leaves.

Cultivation: Endives need an open situation and fertile, moisture-retentive soil. Sow in March and April for the summer crop, and from June to August for the winter crop. Sow either *in situ*, or in a seedbed or in seed trays for transplanting. Sow about 1 cm (½ inch) deep in rows about 30 cm (1 ft) apart, thinning to 30 cm (1 ft) apart. The thinnings can be transplanted carefully to provide a succession.

Plants from the August sowing can be transplanted into an unheated greenhouse, or covered with cloches, for winter use. These will survive most winters, especially if cut for re-sprouting.

The plants are blanched when they are mature. The simplest method of partial blanching is to bunch up the leaves and tie them towards the top of the plant with raffia or an elastic band. This makes the central leaves whiter, and alleviates the bitterness. For complete blanching tie up the leaves when the plant is dry, then cover the plant with a box or plant pot with the drainage holes blocked to exclude light. Alternatively plants can be lifted and planted in a

darkened garden frame. They will be ready for use within 10-15 days. Use immediately otherwise they will start to rot.
Pests and diseases: Endive is usually trouble-free.
Harvesting: Pick individual leaves as required or cut the whole head 2.5 cm (1 inch) above the stem. Leave the stump in the ground as endives will re-sprout over several months, which is most useful in winter and early spring.

LAND CRESS*

Land or American cress is a small plant, with a flavour very similar to watercress. It is exceptionally hardy, so it is particularly useful in winter. In summer it tends to run to seed rapidly in dry weather.

This vegetable tolerates a wide range of soils but does best in rich, fairly moist soil. In summer it can be grown in light shade or intercropped between taller plants.
Cultivation: Sow from March to June for the summer crop and July to September for winter. Sow about 1 cm (½ inch) deep in rows 25 cm (10 inches) apart, thinning to 13 cm (5 inches) apart. For summer sowings water the drills as suggested for corn salad. In autumn protect the plants with cloches, or with bracken or light straw, to keep them in better condition.
Pests and diseases: Flea beetles may attack the seedlings.
Harvesting: The younger leaves are the most tender. Cut leaves as required, leaving the plants to make further growth. Protected plants often provide pickings from autumn until the spring.

LETTUCE*

With careful use of different varieties, lettuces can be available most of the year in much of the country, though it is not easy to produce good quality lettuces in winter.

There are four main types: *Butterheads,* such as 'Unrivalled', have soft, delicate leaves. *Crispheads,* such as 'Webbs Wonderful' and 'Iceberg', have larger crispier leaves but take about three weeks longer to mature. *Cos* lettuce have conical heads and long, sweet, crisp leaves. *'Loose-leaved'* types of lettuce are decorative and non-hearting, but can be picked over a long period.

A particularly sweet, crisp lettuce is 'Little Gem', usually described as a semi-cos. New lettuce varieties are continually appearing, many with useful resistance to diseases.

Cloches are used here to advance early lettuce crops

Lettuces must have fertile soil, an open position, and plenty of moisture throughout the growing season. Being a leafy crop they also need plenty of nitrogen. Prepare the soil by working in plenty of well-rotted manure or compost. A base dressing of a general fertilizer can be given before planting. Lettuces should be rotated to avoid the build up of soil pests and diseases.

Cultivation: Apart from the 'Salad Bowl' type, most lettuces only stand for a short time once they are mature, so frequent sowings must be made. You can sow *in situ* and thin to the correct distance apart, or in seed trays or a seed-bed and transplant. Mid summer sowings, roughly between mid May and mid August, are generally made *in situ* as lettuces transplant badly in hot weather. If the soil is dry at the time of sowing, water the drill first, sow the seed, then cover it with dry soil. This prevents evaporation and lowers the soil temperature, which assists germination in summer. If lettuces are raised in individual soil or peat blocks, which produce excellent plants, they can be transplanted at any time. Seedlings should be planted when they

LETTUCE		
When and how to sow	**Suitable varieties**	**When to harvest**
Early spring sowing (under glass) Sow in cold greenhouses, in frames, or under cloches from mid February in the South, early March in the North. Plant out in early April into frames, under cloches, or in a sheltered position outdoors.	*Loose-leaved: 'Salad Bowl'* *Butterheads: 'Avondefiance', 'Unrivalled', 'Hilde II'* *Cos: 'Little Gem'*	late May and June
Summer sowing Make regular sowings between March and October. To ensure a continuous supply, make the next sowing as soon as the seedlings from the previous sowing have emerged.	*Loose-leaved: 'Salad Bowl'* *Butterheads: 'Avondefiance', 'Continuity', 'Tom Thumb'* *Crispheads: 'Avoncrisp', 'Great Lakes', 'Minetto', 'Windermere'* *Cos: 'Little Gem'*	mid June to mid October
Autumn sowing (with winter protection or warmth) These need transplanting into frames, cold, or slightly heated greenhouses for a winter crop. Sow outdoors initially, and later under cover, from late August until October. Provide ventilation in winter to help prevent disease.	*Winter-maturing varieties: 'Dandie', 'Kwiek', 'Ravel', 'Unrivalled'*	November and December; February and March, depending on temperature
Autumn sowing (to overwinter) These hardy varieties can be overwintered outdoors, or in frames or under cloches, as seedlings. Sow end August or early September, in the open, or under cloches, or in frames, thinning to about 8 cm (3 inches) apart in October, and to the final distance apart in spring. Alternatively, sow in soil or peat blocks. Overwinter in the blocks for planting out in spring.	*Butterheads: 'Imperial Winter', 'Valdor'* *Cos: 'Lobjoits Green', 'Winter Density', 'Little Gem'*	about May

Summer radishes, sown in succession for a constant supply

ave about five leaves, with he seed leaves just above soil evel. Small varieties such as Little Gem' can be 25 cm (9 nches) apart; butterheads bout 30 cm (1 ft) apart, and rispheads and cos up to 35 cm 14 inches) apart.

For a reasonably constant supply of lettuce, follow the sowing plan opposite.

Pests and diseases: Soil pests such as cutworms, leather-ackets, slugs and lettuce root phid can cause serious osses, as can greenfly. The nost serious diseases are bot-ytis and downy mildew, which are worst in cold damp veather. Take usual control neasures (see page 25).

Harvesting: Headed lettuces end to bolt soon after they nature, especially in hot veather. Wherever possible hey should be used in their prime. Make smaller, but suc-essive sowings, if you find ou have too many together.

Some types of lettuce will e-sprout if the heads are cut eaving the stalks in the ground. This is particularly successful in spring with over-wintered varieties and is always worth trying.

The Salad Bowl types of let-uce stand for several months without running to seed. The eaves can either be picked off ndividually as required, or harvested in one by cutting across the head, leaving about .5 cm (¾ inch) of leaf above he stalk. The stalk will throw out further leaves, so allowing a second harvesting a few weeks later, depending on the ime of year.

RADISHES*

There are two sorts of radish: the familiar small summer radishes and the giant winter radishes which are used raw, sliced, or grated, or cooked like turnips. The pods formed when radishes run to seed are also edible and very tasty.

Radishes do best in rich, light, well-drained, sandy soils, with adequate moisture during growth. Use soil manured for a previous crop, and if possible, rotate them with brassicas. The faster they are grown the better; slow-growing radishes become woody and unpleasantly hot.

Good summer varieties are 'Saxa', 'Saxerre', 'Robino', 'Ribella' and 'Cherry Belle' (all these can also be used for early sowings under cloches); and 'French Breakfast', 'Long White Icicle' and 'Red Prince' (which stands very well in summer). Good winter varieties are 'Black Spanish Round', 'China Rose' and 'Mino Early'.

Cultivation: Radishes develop so fast that they are frequently intersown in the same rows as slow-growing crops such as parsnips, or used for inter-cropping. Summer sowings can be made in light shade. For a continuous supply make small, frequent sowings.

Earliest sowings of summer radishes can be made from February onwards under cloches or in frames, followed by outdoor sowings at rough-ly ten-day intervals. Make final sowings under cloches or in a cold greenhouse in September and October.

Sow seed about 2 cm (¾ inch) deep in rows 15 cm (6 inches) apart, spacing the seeds about 4 cm (1½ inches) apart. This avoids the need to thin for, unless radishes are thinned very early, they fail to develop. If the soil is dry when sowing, water the drill heavily beforehand. After sowing, cover the seed with dry soil.

During growth, water suf-ficiently to prevent the soil

drying out, but do not over-water, as this encourages leaf growth at the expense of root.

Winter radishes are sown in July and early August in rows 25 cm (10 inches) apart. Sow very thinly spacing the seeds 5 cm (2 inches) apart, thinning in stages to about 13 cm (5 inches) apart. Given good conditions they can grow up to several pounds in weight!

Pests and diseases: Radish seedlings are sometimes attacked by flea beetles.

Harvesting: Pull summer radishes as required. Winter radishes can be left in the soil protected with straw or bracken. On very heavy soils they may be damaged by slugs: if so store them in a shed in boxes of moist peat or sand. If you want radish pods, leave a plant in the ground to run to seed in spring. Pick the pods when green and crisp, and use fresh in salads or pickle them.

SALAD ROCKET*

Salad, Italian, or Mediterranean rocket, as it is variously known, is a very easily grown and spicily flavoured plant. It is excellent in salads when young, but may become too 'hot' when older, particularly if grown in dry conditions. It can also be cooked as greens.

Cultivation: Salad rocket grows best in the cooler months of early spring and autumn. Sow outdoors from March to early May, and again in September. Mid summer sowings are likely to run to seed rapidly in hot weather.

Prepare the soil, broadcast the seed on the surface and cover with newspaper or plastic film to keep the soil moist until the seeds germinate.

If somewhat larger plants are required seed can also be sown *in situ*, or in seed trays for transplanting, spacing it about 13 cm (5 inches) apart, in rows 25 cm (10 inches) apart.

Pests and diseases: The only likely pest is the flea beetle at the seedling stage.

Harvesting: Pick off the individual leaves as required.

TOMATOES**

Tomatoes need a long season and warm conditions to do well. They can only be grown successfully outdoors in the South of England; elsewhere they are best grown in frames or an unheated greenhouse. A heated greenhouse is only necessary for an exceptionally early crop.

There are numerous varieties, divided into tall, cordon types and dwarf, bush types. The former have to be 'sideshooted' and 'stopped' and require staking, while the bush varieties stop growing naturally and sprawl on the ground, so require no staking.

Wherever it is possible tomatoes should be rotated, and should not be grown near maincrop potatoes, as they are easily infected with potato blight.

On the whole the same varieties can be grown inside and out, though tall varieties, because they make more productive use of the space, are normally used for the greenhouse crop, while bush varieties are generally only grown outdoors. Reliable tall varieties are 'Ailsa Craig', 'Alicante', 'Gardener's Delight' and 'Harbinger'. Reliable bush varieties are the F_1 hybrids 'Sleaford Abundance', 'Alfresco' and 'Pixie', which is a very compact and heavy fruited variety.

Outdoor tomatoes

Cultivation: If possible grow tomatoes against a south-facing wall or erect a windbreak or plastic film screen around them. They can also be grown outdoors in large pots or boxes (using soil-based John Innes No.3 potting compost or a peat-based potting compost), or in growing bags.

Prepare the ground beforehand by working in plenty of well-rotted manure or compost, so that the soil is well-drained but moisture-retentive. A base dressing of a general fertilizer can be applied before planting.

Either raise plants yourself or buy some in, choosing stocky plants, preferably in individual pots. Unfortunately only a few varieties are sold commercially.

If raising your own, sow in gentle heat indoors, in a seed compost, in early April. Prick out the seedlings when they have three leaves into 9 cm (3½) pots, using John Innes No.2 potting compost or a peat-based compost. After hardening off, plant outdoors in late May or early June, after any risk of frost. Plants should be about 20 cm (8 inches) high with the first flower truss showing. Protect them with cloches initially if possible. Plant tall varieties about 38 cm (15 inches) apart, and bush varieties about 45 cm (1½ ft) apart, though if planted a few inches closer they will usually give earlier, but slightly lower, fruit yields.

Mulch plants with plastic to keep them clean, nip out the

sideshoots of tall varieties, and 'stop' them, nipping off the growing point two leaves above a flowering truss, at the end of July or early August.

Tall varieties must be tied to 1.2 metre (4 ft) stakes or horizontal wires attached to posts at either end of the row.

In well-prepared soil outdoor varieties generally need no further feeding. In dry weather water them about twice a week, once they have started flowering, at the rate of about 9 litres/sq metre (2 gallons/sq yd). Overwatering reduces the flavour. Tomatoes in pots or other containers will require more frequent watering, and regular weekly feeding with a proprietary tomato fertilizer.

Tall tomato plant varieties must be secured to stakes for support

Pest and diseases: In wet seasons it may be necessary to spray against potato blight in July and August, using a copper-based fungicide.

Harvesting: Fruits normally start to ripen by the end of August. At the end of September hasten ripening by covering plants with cloches (cut tall varieties off their canes and lay them on the ground). Before frost comes pull up remaining plants by their roots and hang them indoors, or in a greenhouse, to continue ripening.

Greenhouse tomatoes

Cultivation: Tomatoes cannot be grown in the same greenhouse soil for more than three years as the soil becomes diseased. It then either has to be sterilized (which is difficult), or replaced. It is easier to grow tomatoes in pots, bags or boxes in fresh soil or potting compost, or to adopt a soil-less system such as ring culture.

Raise plants as for outdoor tomatoes, sowing in early to mid March and planting in mid to late April. Tie the plants to canes or wire supports, or twist them up strings hung from the roof. Once the first truss has set, feed weekly with a high potash tomato fertilizer. Remove sideshoots from the plants and stop them after seven or eight trusses. Remove yellowing leaves from the base of the plant, and keep the greenhouse well ventilated day and night, to cut down the risk of disease.

Pests and diseases: Uneven watering may cause blossom end rot, which produces sunken patches on the fruits.

Harvesting: Indoor tomatoes can be picked from late July until October or November.

EXOTIC VEGETABLES

Most of our luxurious vegetables are 'exotic' in the strict sense of the word, having been introduced from overseas. It's taking something of a liberty to include in this group seakale, which is a true native, and asparagus, which has grown wild in the British Isles for centuries. Both however, come in the luxury class, partly because they are so delicious and partly because they represent extravagant use of garden space – perennial, spacious vegetables with only a short, but sweet, season of use.

Success with the exotic vegetables depends on how well they have adapted to our climate. The more tender ones, such as aubergines, sweet peppers and sweet corn, can only be grown outdoors in the south, though plant breeders are continually developing hardier varieties. They can also, of course, be grown in greenhouses – heated or unheated.

A little further up the scale, courgettes, marrows and pumpkins have become so established here that they are no longer considered 'foreign', though they cannot be sown outdoors until the risk of frost is past. Globe artichokes, asparagus and asparagus pea present few problems, though globe artichokes may be killed off in severe winters. Perhaps the trickiest customer is Florence fennel, with its tendency to bolt rather than swell up at the base of the stem, in our capricious summers.

There is a slight element of chance in growing the exotics – but they are well worth the effort.

ARTICHOKES, GLOBE*

The Globe artichoke is one of the aristocrats of the kitchen garden, a gourmet's vegetable, and also strikingly handsome with its beautiful silver foliage and thistle-like flowers. The edible parts are the fleshy bases of the scaly bracts enclosing the bud and the 'choke' beneath.

Artichokes are perennial, but they start to deteriorate after their third season, so it is wise to replace a few with new plants each year.

Cultivation: They need fertile, well-drained soil. Prepare the ground by digging in plenty of well-rotted manure or compost. A general fertilizer can be given before planting, or feed them with a seaweed-based fertilizer during growth. Choose an open but not too exposed position, as artichokes cannot withstand severe winters, particularly if growing on heavy soil. A recommended variety for this country is 'Vert de Laon'.

Plants are raised either by planting rooted suckers, known as offsets, or by seed. The former is the more reliable method of obtaining quality artichoke plants.

Either buy offsets between February and April, or take them from the outside edge of a mature established plant. Slice them off cleanly with a spade, making sure you have plenty of root attached to the shoot. Plant them 75 cm (2½ ft) apart each way.

If using seed, sow it indoors in February or outdoors in March, planting in May. The quality will be variable, so build up the stock by taking offsets from the best plants in future years.

During the growing season keep the plants weeded, mulched, and watered so that they do not dry out. The first heads should appear towards the end of summer.

In cold parts of the country, artichokes need some winter protection. Earth up the base of the stems in late autumn and protect the crowns with bracken, dead leaves, or straw. Remove the covering gradually in April.

Pests and diseases: Greenfly and blackfly sometimes attack the developing flower heads.

Harvesting: The artichokes are ready when the buds are nicely plump and the scales still soft. Cut the first main head at the base of the stem, and the secondary heads, which appear later, with about 5 cm (2 inches) of stalk.

ASPARAGUS**

An asparagus bed is a luxury, permanently occupying a fair amount of ground in return for a short, but glorious, season.

Cultivation: A bed should last up to 20 years. Make it on an open site (not where asparagus has previously been grown), avoiding frost

Globe artichokes; the top head is ready for cutting

pockets. Asparagus will grow on a wide range of soils, but the site must be well drained. Traditionally it was grown on raised beds or ridges to ensure good drainage and long white stalks, but today it is usually grown on the flat. The variety 'Giant Mammoth' is recommended for heavy soils: 'Connover's Colossal' for light soils.

To prepare the bed eliminate annual and perennial weeds, using weedkillers if necessary. Then dig in plenty of well-rotted manure or compost the autumn before planting. Very acid soils should be limed.

Asparagus can be raised from seed or purchased as 'crowns'. The quality from seed is more variable, and it takes a year longer to mature, but it can be quite satisfactory. Sow the seed several inches apart 2.5 cm (1 inch) deep in a seed-bed in spring. Leave the plants until the next spring, when the largest should be planted in the bed in the same way as bought crowns.

If starting with asparagus crowns, which look rather like a cross between a spider and octopus, buy one-year, rather than two- or three-year crowns. They become established much better. Dig a trench 30 cm (1 ft) wide and 20 cm (8 inches) deep, and for each plant make a mound a few inches high in the bottom of the trench. Spread the crown on the mound, cover it with 5 cm (2 inches) of soil, and gradually fill in the trench as the shoots grow.

Asparagus can be grown in single rows, or in beds two to three rows wide. Average spacing is 45 cm (1½ ft) between plants. Slightly wider spacing will produce larger spears; closer spacing higher yields of smaller spears.

Weed the beds by hand, or with very shallow hoeing, as the roots are easily damaged. If the 'fern' is falling over in autumn, support it with string attached to canes. Resist the temptation to cut the fern for flower arrangements: it robs the future crop! When the fern dies down naturally, cut the stems 2.5 cm (1 inch) above ground level. Contrary to popular belief, there is no need to mulch or apply salt to the beds during the winter. However, they can be given a general fertilizer in spring (preferably high in nitrogen and potash) or a seaweed-based fertilizer during growth.

Pests and diseases: Slugs can be a major problem in some gardens. The grubs and adults of the asparagus beetle – which has orange marks on a black body – attack stems and foliages. Spray with derris if they are noticed.

Harvesting: Asparagus should not be cut until its third season – two years after planting. Using a sharp knife cut the spears, 13-18 cm (5-7 inches) long, about 2.5 cm (1 inch) below ground. Once the bed is established start cutting the asparagus in April and continue for about eight weeks; but stop after six weeks in the first cutting season.

Asparagus peas with their triangular-shaped winged pods

ASPARAGUS PEA*

The asparagus pea is such a pretty plant it would not come amiss in any flower border. It grows 30-45 cm (1-1½ ft) high, has scarlet-brown pea-like flowers and dainty leaves. It is grown for the curious triangular-shaped winged pods, which have an asparagus flavour – hence the name.

Cultivation: Asparagus peas require rich, light soil in an open situation. Either sow the seeds indoors in early April, planting outside in May, or sow *in situ* in mid April and May. In this case sow several seeds at 'stations' 38 cm (15 inches) apart, thinning to one per station. Protect the plants from pigeons, and give them a little support with twigs, to prevent the pods becoming soiled on the ground. The plants do not crop heavily, so sow several rows if a plentiful supply is required.

Pests and diseases: Serious problems are unlikely.

Harvesting: The delicate flavour is lost if the pods are allowed to become large and tough. Pick the pods when they are no more than 5 cm (2 inches) long, and cook them whole. Regular picking encourages further production, the season lasting from about June to August.

AUBERGINES***

Aubergines are among the most striking looking vegetables. The large pendulous fruits are normally a deep purple-black, but there are white forms such as the variety 'Easter Egg', which look uncommonly like hens' eggs, and presumably gave rise to the alternative name for aubergines – eggplant. The stems and leaves are covered with sharp little spines.

As it is a tropical plant, aubergines do best in a greenhouse, heated in the early stages. They can be grown outdoors in the South, but always choose a sheltered site in full sun, and protect with cloches in the early stages.

Cultivation: Aubergines are demanding plants, so avoid poor, shallow soils. Dig in plenty of well-rotted manure or compost before planting, and make sure the plants have plenty of moisture throughout their growing season.

Sow seed in a greenhouse in gentle heat in March or early April, provided that a minimum night temperature of 16°C (60°F) and day temperature of 18°C (65°F) can be maintained. When the seedlings are about 5 cm (2 inches) high, pot them up in 8 cm (3 inch) pots. Plant them in their permanent positions when the first flower truss is visible, generally in April or May. Do not plant them outdoors until there is no risk of frost, in late May or early June depending on the region. Harden them off well beforehand.

Plant them about 43 cm (17 inches) apart. Aubergines can grow very large and top-heavy, so should either be staked or tied to some kind of support. To encourage sturdy rather than spindly growth, nip out the growing point when the plant is about 38 cm (15 inches) high.

It is best to allow only four fruits to develop on each plant. Each plant has several stems, so once fruits have set, remove all the largest ones on each stem. From then on the plants can be fed with a tomato fertilizer approximately every ten days.

Pests and diseases: When grown indoors aubergines are liable to be attacked by red spider mites, greenfly and whitefly. Syringe the plants frequently with water to keep the atmosphere damp and discourage red spider; try interplanting with French marigolds, which seems to deter aphids and whitefly. Otherwise take routine control measures (see page 24).

Harvesting: Aubergines need a long season to mature, and are not normally ready until late summer. Pick them when they look plump and glossy. If frost threatens, uproot the plants and hang them indoors; fruits will keep for a few weeks on the plant.

Ripe aubergines with their shiny dark purple skins

COURGETTES AND MARROWS*

Marrows are old English favourites, but courgettes, which are nothing more than marrows picked small, young and immature, are a relatively new 'discovery'. (The word courgette is the French for 'little marrow'.) There are many different types of marrow: green, white, yellow, striped, and long, round, cylindrical, or fluted in shape. In the United States, various unusual types of marrows are known as summer squash.

The plants can either be trailing, in which case they can grow several yards long, spreading over the ground, or a compact bush. Although bushes can be a metre (yard) across, they are the most suitable form for small gardens. Recommended varieties for marrows are 'Long Green Trailing', and the bush types 'Green Bush – Small pak'. For courgettes, the F_1 hybrid bushes 'Burpeed Golden Zucchini', 'Chefini', 'Early Gem' and 'Zucchini' are good varieties.

Cultivation: All marrows need an open site, well-drained and very fertile soil, and plenty of moisture throughout growth. Prepare the ground beforehand by digging holes, about 30 cm (1 ft) deep and the same width. Fill them with well-rotted strawy manure and then cover with about 15 cm (6 inches) of soil.

Marrows grow very rapidly but cannot be planted outdoors until the risk of frost is over, so there is little advantage in sowing very early. For planting in frames, under cloches or in a cold greenhouse, sow single seeds, 2 cm (¾) deep, on their sides in small pots, or soil or peat blocks, in early April. Plant them in late April or early May. For the main outdoor crop sow in the same way in late April or early May, planting in late May or early June, after hardening off.

Marrows can also be sown outdoors *in situ* in late May under jars or cloches. Sow two or three seeds together about 2 cm (¾ inch) deep, on their side, and cover with a jam jar to assist germination. Alternatively use cloches for protection. Remove the jars when the seeds have germinated; take the cloches away when they are outgrown.

Bush varieties should be grown 90 cm (3 ft) apart; trailing varieties 1.2 metres (4 ft) apart. Keep the plants well watered, watering more heavily once flowers appear and fruits are forming.

The plants bear separate male and female flowers,

Courgettes – simply small, sweet tender marrows

which are distinguished by the tiny, embryonic marrows behind the flower. Male flowers often appear long before the female. Marrows are insect pollinated and in cold summers, when insects lie low, it may be necessary to hand pollinate by picking off a male flower and rubbing the pollen into the female flower.

Pests and diseases: Powdery mildew is a very disfiguring disease in some seasons. Slugs may also be troublesome.

Harvesting: Start picking courgettes when about 10 cm (4 inches) long; keep picking regularly to encourage further fruiting. The season lasts from mid June until October.

Start picking marrows when they are about 20 cm (8 inches) long. If marrows are required for storage leave a few on the plant so that they grow larger and their skins harden, then hang them in nets in a dry, frost-free shed. They may keep until about Christmas.

Florence fennel needs a fairly warm summer to grow well

FENNEL**

Florence or sweet fennel is a beautiful, feathery-leaved plant grown for the swollen bulb at the base of the stem – though it may be admitted that in our climate it is sometimes reluctant to form the much-prized bulb. Fennel can be used cooked or raw, but the delicate aniseed flavour is most marked when eaten raw. Florence fennel should not be confused with the hardier, perennial fennel, which is grown as a herb.

Cultivation: Fennel likes much the same conditions as celery, and like celery, is liable to bolt if subjected to spells of very cold or very dry weather, or, because of its susceptibility to different day lengths, if sown too early in the year. Varieties least likely to bolt are 'Perfection' and 'Zefa Fino'.

Although fennel can be grown on heavy soil, it does best on fertile, light, well-drained soil, requiring plenty of moisture throughout its growth. Work in plenty of well-rotted manure or compost before planting.

Seed can be sown 1 cm (½ inch) deep, *in situ* outdoors, or in small pots or soil or peat blocks indoors, for planting out after hardening off. Make several sowings if a succession is required. The earliest sowings can be made in April and May, but because of the likelihood of bolting, these are something of a gamble. The main sowings are made in June and early July, and a late sowing from mid July until early August. These last can be planted into a cold greenhouse or frames to give a late autumn crop.

Plant out when seedlings are about 10-13 cm (4-5 inches) high, spacing the plants about 30 cm (1 ft) apart each way. Early plantings will benefit

Sweet peppers require a sheltered outdoor position

from cloche protection if the weather is cold or windy. Take precautions against slugs in the early stages, and keep the plants well watered and mulched. Feed them from time to time with a seaweed-based fertilizer. The faster they grow the better!

Although by no means essential, the bulb is traditionally blanched by earthing it up when it starts to swell. Pull earth up a few inches around the base.

Pests and diseases: Fennel is usually trouble-free.

Harvesting: Depending on sowing times, the season can last from July to November. Cut the bulb about 2 cm (¾ inch) above the ground rather than uprooting the plant. It will often throw out further small shoots which are pleasant in salads or for flavouring cooked dishes.

PEPPERS, SWEET AND CHILLI**

Both the rather 'boxy' sweet peppers and the long, hot chilli peppers can be grown in this country. Sweet peppers are generally used in their immature green state, but in hot summers they will mature and turn red. Mature red peppers have a milder, sweeter flavour than green ones. Like aubergines, peppers require a warm climate, and are only successful outdoors in the South, preferably with cloche protection until the cloches are outgrown. Elsewhere they must be grown in frames or unheated greenhouses.

Peppers are easier to grow than aubergines, tolerating slightly lower temperatures and less fertile conditions, and needing a shorter growing season. The F_1 hybrid sweet peppers 'Ace', 'Canape' and 'Early Prolific' are recommended for early maturity.

Cultivation: Prepare the ground, in a sheltered spot outdoors or in a greenhouse, by working in well-rotted manure or compost. Peppers can also be grown in pots or growing bags like tomatoes.

Sow seed in a greenhouse in gentle heat in March or early April, provided that a minimum night temperature of 15°C (60°C) and day temperature of 18°C (65°F) can be maintained. When the seedlings are about 5 cm (2 inches) high, pot them up in 8 cm (3 inch) pots. Plant them in their permanent positions when the first flower truss is visible, generally in April or May.

If the plant is growing weakly when the first central flower appears, remove to encourage the development of side-shoots. If the plant is vigorous at the time it can be left.

Do not plant them outdoors until there is no risk of frost, in late May or early June depending on the region. Harden them off well beforehand.

Plant them about 43 cm (17 inches) apart. Water regularly to prevent the soil drying out, mulch the plants and protect against pests. Feed with a tomato fertilizer approximately every ten days. Stake the plants if they show signs of being top-heavy.

Pests and diseases: Red spider mites, green fly, and whitefly can all be a problem.

Harvesting: Peppers can carry a surprisingly large number of fruits. Start picking when the first peppers are the size of a tennis ball, and keep picking regularly to encourage further cropping. Before frost threatens pull up the plants by their roots. Chillis can be hung in a kitchen until required. Sweet peppers will keep in reasonable condition on the plants for several months in a frost-free, cool, dry place.

PUMPKINS*

The term pumpkin embraces those gourds which can be used fresh or stored for winter, known in the United States as 'winter squash'. Most popular in this country is the giant, orange, pumpkin – but there are many others.

Pumpkins are extremely vigorous, and provided the roots are in fertile soil, they can be effective ground-cover plants in unsightly corners, blanketing a fairly large area of ground during the growing season.

Cultivation: Grow pumpkins like outdoor marrows, planting them about 1.2 metre (4 ft) apart. Mark the plants with canes when planting, otherwise it is hard to find the roots for watering when the stems spread. If large pumpkins are required, limit the fruits to three or four to each plant, picking off surplus flowers. Remove all growths beyond the fruits once they have set.

Pests and diseases: Powdery mildew and slugs are likely to be the main problems.

Harvesting: Pumpkins earmarked for storage should be left on the plant as long as possible, removing any leaves that are shading them. Cut them off in the autumn before night frosts are expected, and leave them in a sunny spot against a wall for several days for the skins to colour up and harden. Store them on shelves, or if not too heavy, suspended in nets in a frost-free, dry shed or cellar. They should keep in good condition until the following spring.

Pumpkins can be grown to large proportions in fertile soil

SEAKALE**

Although considered an old-fashioned vegetable, the subtle, nutty flavour and crisp texture of blanched seakale stalks in spring is a treat. Seakale is perennial, and once established is productive for eight to ten years.

Cultivation: Prepare an open site by working in plenty of well-rotted manure or compost. Buy plants or rooted cuttings (thongs); alternatively raise plants from seed or from your own thongs.

Sow fresh seed (old seed germinates poorly) in a seedbed in spring. Keep the ground moist until the seed germinates. Plant seedlings into their permanent position in autumn, 30 cm (1 ft) apart each way. Alternatively sow *in situ* in rows 30 cm (1 ft) apart, thinning to 30 cm (1 ft) apart.

Thongs are obtained by lifting plants that are at least three years old in the autumn. Select roots of finger thickness, and cut them into pieces 10-15 cm (4-6 inches) long. Trim them flat across the top and with a slanting cut across the bottom, so that you know which end is which! Store these upright in a box of moist sand until early March, when buds will have formed. Rub out weak buds leaving one strong central bud, and plant the thongs outdoors in spring.

Water so that the ground does not dry out in the summer. Allow the plants to grow undisturbed for their first two seasons, feeding them occasionally with a seaweed-based fertilizer. If they have many feeble shoots thin them out to encourage stronger shoots. In late autumn remove dead leaves from the base of the plant and cover the crowns with a little soil.

Pests and diseases: If there is clubroot in the ground, this vegetable is likely to be affected.

Harvesting: Plants are ready for blanching in their third season. The simplest method is to cover the plants with 30 cm (1 ft) high buckets or plant pots, with the drainage hole blocked to exclude light, in January. The whitened shoots can be cut in late March and April. Stop cutting in May and remove the buckets or pots, so that they can continue to grow naturally.

Plants can be forced indoors for winter. Wait until the first frost, then lift and pot up the crowns in peat, covering them with a flower pot to exclude the light. Bring them into a temperature of 16-21°C (60-70°F). After forcing, the crown is exhausted, and if planted out again will take several years to recover.

Seakale is well worth growing for its delicate nutty flavour

SWEET CORN**

Sweet corn or corn-on-the-cob is an increasingly popular vegetable, but it is tender and needs a long, warm summer, so becomes progressively harder to grow the further north one is. Early-maturing hybrid varieties such as 'Earliking', 'Kelvedon Sweetheart' and 'Northern Belle' are to be recommended.

Cultivation: Avoid exposed sites and very heavy or very dry soil. Sweet corn does best on well-drained, reasonably fertile soil, preferably manured for the previous crop.

It cannot be planted outside until there is no risk of frost (in late May or early June, depending on the area) so is normally sown indoors for transplanting. However, the young plants dislike root disturbance, so where possible sow seed in small pots of potting compost, or soil or peat blocks, rather than in seed trays.

Sow about 2.5 cm (1 inch) deep in April in gentle heat, sowing two or three seeds to each block or pot, thinning later to one seedling. Plant out, under cloches if possible, after hardening off. Sweet corn should be grown in blocks rather than single rows, to assist with wind pollination – so space them 35 cm (14 inches) apart each way, several plants deep.

In the South seeds can be sown *in situ*, preferably warming the soil first with cloches, or sowing two or three seeds at each 'station' under a jam-jar or cloche, thinning to one seedling after germination. Seed will not germinate until the soil temperature reaches 10°C (50°F), so it is generally unwise to sow outside until early May.

Sweet corn is easily 'rocked' by wind, so when the plants are 30-45 cm (1-1½ ft) high, earth up the stems, much as one earths up potatoes, to a height of several inches. Weed by hand if necessary, taking care not to disturb the shallow roots. Once the plants are flowering, water, if the weather is dry, at the rate of 22 litres/sq metre (4 gallons/sq yd) every few days. This increases the yield and improves the quality.

Sweet corn; the visible cob is ready for cutting

Pests and diseases: Sweet corn is usually trouble-free.

Harvesting: Expect only one or two cobs on each plant. They are ripe when the tassels are turning brown and the cobs are at a 45 degree angle to the stem and snap off easily. If a finger nail is pressed into the kernel the juice is watery when under-ripe, 'doughy' when over-ripe, and milky when ripe. Harvest immediately, otherwise the sweetness is lost.

INDEX

ACKNOWLEDGMENTS

Special Photography by Neil Holmes

All illustrations by Josephine Martin, except those on pages 6, 24-5 drawn by Patti Pearce. Both artists from The Garden Studio.

The publishers wish to thank the following individuals and organisations for their kind permission to reproduce the photographs in this book:
A-Z Botanical 27; Michael Boys/Octopus 2; Jerry Harpur/Octopus 43; Harry Smith Horticultural Photographic Collection 31; Michael Warren 34-35; George Wright/Octopus half title.

The publishers would also like to thank RHS Gardens, Wisley, for their help with location photography.